Charles Dickens'

Hard Times

Text by
Oliver Conant
(M. Phil., Columbia University)
Department of English
Kean College
New York, New York

Illustrations by
Michael Kupka

 Research & Education Association

MAXnotes® for
HARD TIMES

Printed in the United States of America

Library of Congress Catalog Card Number 96-67447

International Standard Book Number 0-87891-016-6

MAXnotes® is a registered trademark of
Research & Education Association, Piscataway, New Jersey 08854

What **MAXnotes®** *Will Do for You*

This book is intended to help you absorb the essential contents and features of Charles Dickens' *Hard Times* and to help you gain a thorough understanding of the work. The book has been designed to do this more quickly and effectively than any other study guide.

For best results, this **MAXnotes** book should be used as a companion to the actual work, not instead of it. The interaction between the two will greatly benefit you.

To help you in your studies, this book presents the most up-to-date interpretations of every section of the actual work, followed by questions and fully explained answers that will enable you to analyze the material critically. The questions also will help you to test your understanding of the work and will prepare you for discussions and exams.

Meaningful illustrations are included to further enhance your understanding and enjoyment of the literary work. The illustrations are designed to place you into the mood and spirit of the work's settings.

The **MAXnotes** also include summaries, character lists, explanations of plot, and section-by-section analyses. A biography of the author and discussion of the work's historical context will help you put this literary piece into the proper perspective of what is taking place.

The use of this study guide will save you the hours of preparation time that would ordinarily be required to arrive at a complete grasp of this work of literature. You will be well prepared for classroom discussions, homework, and exams. The guidelines that are included for writing papers and reports on various topics will prepare you for any added work which may be assigned.

The **MAXnotes** will take your grades "to the max."

Dr. Max Fogiel
Program Director

Contents

**Each Chapter includes List of Characters,
Summary, Analysis, Study Questions and
Answers, and Suggested Essay Topics.**

SECTION ONE

Introduction

The Life and Work of Charles Dickens

Charles Dickens is one of the most popular and beloved writers who ever lived. His novels and tales catered to a vast and intensely loyal audience. More than just an entertainer, Dickens used his enormous popularity to attack injustice and strengthen the sympathies of his readers for the poor and the helpless, for orphans and outcast persons.

Charles John Huffham Dickens was born in 1812, near Portsmouth, England, to a family in the middle-class. His father was a minor government official, a clerk in the navy's pay office; his paternal grandmother had been in domestic service, as a housekeeper. In his boyhood, Dickens' family experienced money troubles. For a time, his father was even imprisoned for debt in London's Marshalsea Prison. His wife and younger children accompanied him to the prison. But Dickens, the second eldest of eight children, was expected to work to help the family. He was pulled out of school, and, at the age of 12, sent to work in a factory warehouse, pasting labels on bottles of blacking (shoe polish) for six shillings a week.

Dickens' father was eventually released and Dickens resumed his schooling. For the proud, sensitive boy, who had dreamed of becoming a distinguished gentleman, the whole experience had been a terrible, humiliating, lonely ordeal. It profoundly affected him, haunted his writing (most notably in the autobiographical *David Copperfield*), and colored his view of the world.

At 15, Dickens left school to become a clerk in a law office. After teaching himself shorthand, he became a legal reporter, and covered debates in Parliament for the newspapers. His skepticism about organized politics and established institutions probably dates from this time in his life.

In 1837, when he was only 25, *Pickwick Papers* was published. His first novel, it was an enormous success with the public. It was issued in installments, as a serial, as were the rest of his novels, including *Hard Times*, which appeared in 1854. Writing his novels in this way, in cheap monthly or weekly parts (called "numbers") was somewhat confining to Dickens' creative freedom. But it also allowed for an extraordinary closeness between Dickens and his readers and made him into an expert at "cliff-hanger" endings. His audience (which, of course, had no movies or TV soap operas to distract it) was kept in suspense, impatient to discover what happened to the characters in the next "number."

Dickens' fame came early and never left him. He worked tirelessly to sustain it, and to support the 10 children given him by his wife, Catherine Hogarth, the genteel daughter of one of Dickens' newspaper editors. In early years riches eluded him, but in later life his novels paid handsomely, and he was able to purchase a mansion in the country, Gads Hill Place. This was the very house that in his childhood his father had often pointed out to him on their walks together, telling him that if he worked hard he might hope to live there one day.

The glittering success Dickens had made of his life, its seeming vindication of his society's beliefs about the value of perseverance and hard work, still left him in many ways unsatisfied and restless within himself. In 1858 his marriage to Catherine, never entirely happy, ended in a separation, and he began a relationship with an actress, Ellen Lawless Ternan, who was many years his junior. The happy marriages with which so many of his novels end are offset by acute descriptions, notably in evidence in *Hard Times*, of bad marriages and unhappy homes.

Dickens often spoke out on public affairs and became involved with a variety of causes such as prison reform and the abolition of the death penalty. In 1842 he visited America, and although sympathetic to the young republic, was forthright in criticizing its failings, particularly the evil of slavery. In England he lent his active support to a variety of philanthropic endeavors. The problem of the education of the poor, and of children particularly, engaged his attention. Along with its focus on the evils of the industrial system, education is a major theme of *Hard Times*.

Hard Times sold well, significantly boosting the circulation of the weekly magazine (founded and edited by Dickens himself), in which it first appeared. The critical reception was mixed. Dickens' accounts of industrial life and his satirical treatment of political economists were attacked by critics with a stake in the debate; the popular journalist and adherent of laissez-faire economics Harriet Martineau, for example, found it "unlike life...master and man are as unlike life in England, at present, as Ogre and Tom Thumb." But John Ruskin, the great Victorian art critic and sage, thought *Hard Times* the greatest of Dickens' works, and wrote that it "should be studied with close and earnest care by persons interested in social questions." Nearer to our own time, figures as different as George Bernard Shaw and Sigmund Freud have testified to its power. In his book *The Great Tradition*, the influential English critic F. R. Leavis asserted that *Hard Times* is "a masterpiece," which (according to Leavis) unlike any of his other novels has the strength of a "completely serious work of art."

Toward the end of his life, Dickens threw himself into a series of highly dramatic public readings of his works. While remunerative, these were emotionally draining and contributed to his declining health. He died in 1870. Universally mourned, he was buried in the Poet's Corner of Westminster Abbey.

After Shakespeare, Dickens is the most written about author in English literature. Dickens' 14 major novels, and numerous shorter works such as *A Christmas Carol*, brim with humor, satire, and pathos; they teem with a fantastic array of entertaining characters and convey vividly and memorably a sense of the author's times: its hopes and sorrows, follies and pleasures, houses and streets, factories and schools, manners and people. In one way or another they all also show Dickens' intense concern with the injustices of his society. Some of these continue to beset us in our own, very different, time; this is one of the reasons why Dickens' work still speaks to us to this day.

Historical Background

The period in which Dickens wrote is called the Victorian Age, after the popular, long-lived Queen Victoria, who occupied the throne of England from 1837—the very year Dickens made his debut in fiction—until 1901.

Victorian England was the scene of enormous, far-reaching changes: changes in the nature and organization of work, in population growth, and changes in the very landscape itself, brought about by the railway and the growth of wholly new industrial cities and towns like the Coketown described in *Hard Times*.

In 1812, when Dickens was born, England had a largely agricultural economy and a population of around nine million. The great majority passed their lives in the country, working the fields and farms as their ancestors had done before them. A small class of landowners held much of the political power, presiding over a small electorate of propertied men. Although the American and French Revolutions had occurred recently enough to be a living memory, England in 1812 felt itself to be, and to some extent was, continuous with the England of past ages, a hierarchical society based on hereditary privilege with unquestioned traditions, beliefs, and a settled order.

By 1854, however, the year Dickens published *Hard Times*, conditions were quite different. Half the people lived in towns or cities, and there were vastly more of them: in 1851, when a census was taken, the population had passed the 17 million mark. Marvelous new machines, like the power loom operated by the character Stephen Blackpool, replaced many tasks formerly performed by hand, increasing the country's productivity but also causing unrest and unemployment. For the toilers in the factories—a shocking number of whom were children—traditional rural ways were being left behind for repetitive, monotonous, and often health-destroying new routines of work.

Whenever humanitarian objections were raised to conditions in their factories, the new class of industrialists—caricatured in *Hard Times* in the person of Josiah Bounderby—often turned to the doctrines of political economy, especially the idea of "laissez faire," and the "hardheaded" outlook of Utilitarianism. In *Hard Times*, Bounderby's friend and ally Thomas Gradgrind is shown upholding some of the views, heavily satirized by Dickens, of political economy and Utilitarianism.

By 1854, portions of England's working class had formed into "combinations" (unions), which used strikes or the threat of strikes as a way to force employers to improve wages and conditions. Working-class militancy in England had its nineteenth-century origin in a movement called Chartism, which in the 1830s and 1840s called for an electoral bill of rights, including universal manhood suffrage (the right to vote for all adult males, with no qualification of property). Dickens' response to Chartism, like that of many in the middle classes, was ambivalent; he sympathized with the sufferings and the hunger that motivated workers but feared the potential for violence and social disorder accompanying Chartist agitation. The rhetoric of working-class protest, freely borrowed from radical Republican and Christian (Protestant) sources, is mocked in *Hard Times* in the speeches of Slackbridge, the union leader.

In the intellectual and cultural spheres, the England of 1854 was a very different place from the one Dickens was born into. New and disturbing challenges to old certainties were in the air; Darwin's evolutionary ideas were soon to undermine religious faith, and new ideologies like socialism questioned the entire basis of the social order. In the arts, the movement called Romanticism had entered into the feelings, and changed the outlook, of many who believed—Dickens was one—in the importance of cultivating the imagination and in the central place childhood holds in human development. For them, the Romantic poet William Blake's image of the "dark Satanic Mills" appeared frighteningly apt for places like Coketown.

Master List of Characters

Thomas Gradgrind—*a citizen of Coketown, proprietor of a model school, member of Parliament, father of Tom and Louisa.*

Mrs. Gradgrind—*Thomas Gradgrind's ailing, complaining wife. She is a victim as much as her children to her husband's regimen of Fact.*

Tom Gradgrind—*Thomas Gradgrind's selfish, ne'er-do-well son, called "the whelp," employed in Bounderby's bank.*

Louisa Gradgrind—*Thomas Gradgrind's eldest daughter. She is disastrously married to the much older industrialist Josiah Bounderby.*

Mr. James Harthouse—*a dilettante friend of Gradgrind's. He makes love to Louisa.*

Sissy (Cecilia) Jupe—*a tender-hearted pupil at Gradgrind's school.*

Josiah Bounderby—*a blustering mill owner and banker who boasts constantly of being a self-made man.*

Mrs. Sparsit—*a well-born, snobbish but impoverished widow. She is employed by Bounderby as his housekeeper.*

Lady Scadgers—*great aunt to Mrs. Sparsit.*

Bitzer—*a model pupil, employed by Bounderby as a porter (and informer). He hates Tom Gradgrind and tries to have him arrested for theft.*

Mr. M'Choakumchild—*an overzealous teacher in Gradgrind's school.*

Mr. Sleary—*the owner and manager of "Sleary's Horse-Riding," a traveling circus.*

Signor Jupe—*Sissy's father, a melancholy clown in Sleary's Circus.*

Josephine Sleary—*Mr. Sleary's daughter and a circus performer.*

Mr. E.W.B. Childers—*a performer who is the "Wild Huntsman of the North American Prairies" in Sleary's Circus.*

Master Kidderminster—*Mr. Childers' son and partner, "a diminutive boy with an old face."*

Mr. Slackbridge—*the speechifying leader of Coketown's factory operatives.*

Stephen Blackpool—*an honest factory hand. He is unhappily married, ostracized by Slackbridge and his fellow workers, and unjustly accused of robbery. He dies after falling down a disused mine shaft on his way back to Coketown.*

Rachael—*a factory hand. She is a friend to Stephen, whom he would have married had not the law prevented him from divorcing his fallen, drunken wife.*

Stephen's wife—*an unnamed, drunken, sub-human woman.*

Mrs. Pegler—*a mysterious old woman from the country who turns out to be Bounderby's mother.*

Summary of the Novel

Thomas Gradgrind, a citizen of the northern industrial town of Coketown, is a convinced Utilitarian: an enemy to Fancy and a worshiper of Fact. He is intent on having the pupils in his model school—who include his children, Tom and Louisa—crammed so full of knowledge as to leave no room for anything else.

Two other pupils of Gradgrind's prove important to the story: the naturally affectionate Sissy Jupe, the daughter of a performer in Sleary's Circus (a traveling troupe of clowns, jugglers, and horseback riders), and Bitzer, an emotionless, eerily pale boy who absorbs all of Gradgrind's precepts. When Sissy's father abandons her, Gradgrind takes her into his household, making her a companion to his ailing wife. Sissy turns out to be a faithful friend to Louisa and Tom; the calculating, cold-hearted Bitzer, her opposite, turns on his old mentor in the end.

When she comes of age, Louisa marries her father's friend and ally Josiah Bounderby, a boastful, bullying Coketown manufacturer and banker, who claims, untruthfully, to be an entirely self-made man, abandoned by his mother at an early age and reared in the street. Louisa marries Bounderby despite their difference in age (he is some 30 years her senior) and not loving him in the slightest. She takes this disastrous step for several reasons: because it is her father's view that between his daughter and Mr. Bounderby there is "great suitability" of "means and positions"; because she wishes to ensure Bounderby's approval of her beloved younger brother, who has been hired as a clerk at Bounderby's bank; and finally, because her rearing has left her so lacking in any genuine feeling (apart, that is, from her passionate devotion to her brother), that she doesn't care what becomes of her.

Her brother, Tom, himself emotionally deprived and deeply selfish, barely acknowledges his sister's self-sacrifice. To pay his gambling debts, he steals from Bounderby's bank and tries to throw suspicion onto Stephen Blackpool, an honest power loom operator in Bounderby's mill.

The attempted frame-up is only the latest in a series of afflictions suffered by Blackpool. Chained to a drunken wife his circumstances do not allow him to divorce, Blackpool has been ostracized by Slackbridge, the union leader, for refusing to join the other operatives in a strike over conditions (previously Blackpool had promised Rachael, a fellow worker and the woman he loves, that he would steer clear of all industrial conflicts). After a memorable confrontation with Bounderby, Blackpool leaves Coketown, despised by masters and men alike. He dies after falling down a disused mine shaft while returning to Coketown to try to clear his name of the charge of robbery.

Louisa, meanwhile, has come increasingly under the spell of James Harthouse, an amoral, handsome, young upper-class gentleman who contrasts favorably with her vulgar husband. When Tom's guilt is discovered and Louisa runs away from her husband—not with Harthouse, but back to her father, whom she bitterly denounces for having crippled her capacity to feel—the failure of his educational system is brought home to Gradgrind. The outraged Bounderby is forced to accept a separation and the further humiliation of being publicly exposed by his mother. In the end, Louisa is able (unlike Blackpool) to secure a separation from her unsuitable partner, Sissy Jupe intervenes to ward off Harthouse, and Tom, avoiding arrest and the grimly pursuing Bitzer, flees the country with the timely aid of Sleary's Circus.

Estimated Reading Time

Hard Times is divided into three books, with 37 chapters of varying length. The whole is considerably shorter than other novels by Dickens. Assuming the student can read four to five chapters at a sitting, a period of two weeks should be enough time to finish the novel.

Hard Times, Book I: Reaping

Chapter 1: The One Thing Needful
Chapter 2: Murdering the Innocents

New Characters:

Thomas Gradgrind: *the proprietor of a model school*

Mr. M'Choakumchild: *the school teacher*

Unnamed "Government Officer": *present to inspect schools*

Bitzer: *a model pupil*

Sissy Jupe: *another pupil, who answers inappropriately*

Summary

In a plain, bare classroom, students sit in rows, listening to a speaker, a square-faced man who lectures them on the all-importance of Fact. This is Mr. Thomas Gradgrind, a "man of Realities, a man of facts and calculation." He is accompanied in the classroom by two other adults: his school teacher, Mr. M'Choakumchild, a recent graduate of the new state-supported teacher training, and an unnamed man, a "government officer," apparently inspecting the school in his official capacity.

Gradgrind calls on Sissy Jupe (as "girl number 20"), asks for her name and what her father does for a living, ascertains that he

is one of the "horse riders" (performers) in Sleary's Circus, and asks for her "definition of a horse." Sissy is unable to give him the answer, but another student, the boy Bitzer, answers in the approved style: "Quadruped. Graminivorous. Forty teeth, namely twenty-four grinders."

The third man then addresses the children, asking them if they would decorate their houses with patterned wallpaper or cover their floors with flowered carpets. Sissy Jupe is again called upon and answers that she would very much like to decorate her home that way, missing the point that the gentleman is trying to develop, namely that "What is called Taste, is only another name for Fact," and that none of them are to have "any object of use or ornament, what would be a contradiction in fact." You don't, he observes sarcastically, ever actually see horses going up and down walls or butterflies and birds on teapots; therefore, you should not permit these things in your homes.

The floor is then turned over to M'Choakumchild, who delivers his preparatory lesson, which looks to be everything Gradgrind could hope for in the way of a barrage of facts on assorted subjects, but which Dickens does not record.

Analysis

Hard Times opens with an angry speech delivered in a classroom. The manner and emphases of the speech seem better suited to a lecture or meeting hall than a room filled with children. In the second chapter we learn that the speaker, Thomas Gradgrind, is in the habit of addressing everyone in this emphatic, "I won't be contradicted" tone.

The description of the classroom "a plain, bare, monotonous vault," is brief but evocative and is carried over in the description of the speaker: his hardness, dryness, and squareness. All this seems intended to convey, more even than through his words, the hardness and unfeeling nature of Gradgrind's philosophy.

The children are called "little vessels" and "little pitchers." The idea seems to be that they are to be "filled," as a jug is filled with water, with factual knowledge. They are thus considered as entirely passive recipients, and what they learn as external to them.

That Gradgrind addresses Sissy Jupe as "girl number 20" is

significant: it is meant to show how abstractly Gradgrind conceives of other people. His own name, of course, is evocative of what his beliefs have made of him: a sort of human "fact machine," a grinder of fact. (Today's expression "a grind," used for an excessively hard-working student, one who takes no joy in life, is fairly close to what Dickens wished to connote by the name). Other names in the novel are similarly indicative (often satirically) of their holders: "M'Choakumchild" is a typical example.

The title of Chapter 2, "Murdering the Innocents, " is striking. Gradgrind is at one point even compared to a loaded cannon, "prepared to blow [the children] clean out of the regions of childhood at one discharge." The metaphor is intended to underline how much harm Gradgrind is capable of doing. In effect Dickens is accusing Gradgrind of killing the imagination of his pupils.

Study Questions

1. Chapter 1 is entitled "The One Thing Needful." What is that one thing?

2. What does Gradgrind want to "plant" and what does he want to "root out" of his pupils?

3. To whom does Gradgrind say "Sissy is not a name...Don't call yourself Sissy. Call yourself Cecilia."

4. What gesture does Bitzer make once he finishes his answer?

5. What direct comment does the narrator permit himself about the teacher M'Choakumchild?

6. The "government officer" is compared to what kind of professional athlete?

7. Instead of patterned china and wallpaper and flowery carpets, with what does the government officer urge the children to decorate their homes?

8. Which character is said to have been, with 140 others, "turned at the same time, in the same factory, on the same principles, like so many pianoforte legs"?

9. How does the girl Sissy's physical appearance differ from the boy Bitzer's?

10. Which "calling" (occupation) does Gradgrind not wish mentioned in his classroom?

Answers

1. "Facts" are the one thing needful, at least as far as Gradgrind and his associates are concerned. The phrase is meant to suggest the reductiveness of Gradgrind's philosophy.

2. Again, "Facts" are what Gradgrind wishes to plant in the minds of the children; to be rooted out is any suggestion of "Fancy," or imagination.

3. The remark is addressed to Cecilia (Sissy) Jupe.

4. Bitzer knuckles his forehead. This is a traditional lower class gesture, indicating deference to a social superior.

5. "Ah, rather overdone, M'Choakumchild. If he had only learnt a little less, how infinitely better he might have taught much more!"

6. The government officer is compared to a boxer, "ready to fight all England."

7. The government officer says that for purposes of decoration, the children must only use "combinations and modifications (in primary colors) of mathematical figures which are susceptible of proof and demonstration." These figures are, presumably, painted squares and triangles or other geometrical figures.

8. M'Choakumchild is so described. Dickens is saying that the schoolmaster's own education has been a mechanical process, like the manufacture of pianoforte (a type of piano) legs. His extensive training has left him and all those subjected to it identical to one another, lacking any individual traits.

9. Sissy has dark hair and eyes, and her complexion glows in the light of the sun; Bitzer, by contrast, is pale all over and looks as though "if he were cut, he would bleed white."

10. Gradgrind does not wish to hear anything about Sissy Jupe's father's occupation as a circus performer.

Suggested Essay Topics

Suggested Essay Topics

1. Examine Dickens' use of repetition in these two chapters, explaining what you think Dickens gains by repeating such words as "hard," "fact," "sir," "square," and "squarely."

2. Discuss just what Gradgrind and the others appear to *mean* by "facts."

3. Dickens' position appears to be that teachers who are not so well-prepared as M'Choakumchild, who may indeed have learned less than he has, would make better teachers. That, knowing less, they could teach "infinitely" more. Argue for or against this idea, basing your remarks on a combination of what you have observed in your own teachers and what Dickens tells you about M'Choakumchild and Gradgrind's school.

Chapter 3: A Loophole
Chapter 4: Mr. Bounderby

New Characters:

Mr. Sleary: *owner of "Sleary's Horse-Riding," an equestrian circus*

Miss Josephine Sleary: *his daughter, who performs in the circus*

Signor Jupe: *Sissy Jupe's father, who performs with his trained dog, Merrylegs*

Mr. Bounderby: *a wealthy mill owner and banker*

Mrs. Gradgrind: *Thomas Gradgrind's feeble wife*

Adam Smith, Malthus, and Jane Gradgrind: *the younger sons and infant daughter of Thomas Gradgrind*

Summary

Mr. Gradgrind walks from his school to his home, Stone Lodge, built on a moor just outside Coketown, a "great town" in Northern England. He thinks with satisfaction about his school and his children, about how he intends all the pupils in the school to be model pupils, and how he believes his own children to be models of his strictly rational and practical approach to life and learning.

Reaching the outskirts of Coketown on his way home, Mr. Gradgrind hears the unexpected sound of band music from a traveling circus. Mr. Sleary himself can be seen at a ticket booth, and there is a poster identifying his daughter, Josephine, and Sissy Jupe's father as performers. Mr. Gradgrind keeps going, paying no attention. But just then something does grab him: the sight of a group of school-aged children trying to peep into the circus. He puts on his eyeglass and is astonished to find his own Tom and Louisa looking on with the rest.

Mr. Gradgrind asks disapprovingly what they think they are doing there. Louisa says only that she "wanted to see what it was like." But what would their friends think, Gradgrind asks reproachfully. What would Mr. Bounderby think?

As it happens, Mr. Bounderby himself is waiting for them at Stone Lodge, having dropped by to call on his old friend—and on Louisa. What he thinks about the circus episode is exactly what Mr. Gradgrind thinks—it seems they always agree perfectly.

A large, loud bald man in late middle-age, he is standing near the drawing-room fireplace telling Thomas Gradgrind's invalid wife the story of his early life, when Gradgrind, Tom and Louisa return. Bounderby hits on a practical explanation for Tom and Louisa's behavior and has a practical solution to propose. His explanation is that they must have been lured out to look at the circus people by their classmate, Sissy Jupe, who Bounderby has heard is "one of those stroller's children," and his solution is to have the girl kicked out of the school, right away. Gradgrind has Sissy's father's address and invites Bounderby to accompany him to Coketown to tell the father his daughter must leave.

While Gradgrind goes upstairs for the address, Bounderby walks into the children's study, requests a kiss from Louisa, plants one on her "ungraciously" offered cheek, and sets forth with Mr. Gradgrind on their errand.

Analysis

These two chapters move outward from the confinement of Gradgrind's classroom and into Gradgrind's world: Stone Lodge,

his house on the edge of Coketown, his relations with his family and they with him, and his great friend Bounderby. Gradgrind's home life is a dismal affair. His wife, whom he seems to have married for money, is practically an idiot, entirely absorbed in her own ailments, a "little, thin, white, pink-eyed bundle of shawls, of surpassing feebleness, mental and bodily" who "whenever she showed a symptom of coming to life, was invariably stunned by some weighty piece of fact tumbling on her." The younger Gradgrinds—whose numbers include two named after Adam Smith, the great economist, and Thomas Malthus, the Utilitarian philosopher—have had their own childhoods taken away from them. They have never read a story book, never learned a nursery rhyme, "never known wonder."

Gradgrind is not an ill-intentioned or evil man—Dickens even calls him "an affectionate father, after his manner." But he is a prisoner to his system, unable to understand his own children. Their desire to see the circus—which anyone else would think perfectly normal—utterly baffles him.

Of Gradgrind's daughter Louisa, we learn that she is a girl of 15 or 16, soon to be a woman, pretty, with an air of "jaded sullenness" that she shares with her younger brother. She gives her father a "searching look" when he asks her what Mr. Bounderby would think of her peeping at the circus, a look that, characteristically, her father misses. In fact there appears to be active dislike on Louisa's part for Bounderby.

With his "great puffed head and forehead, swelled veins in his temples" and the "pervading appearance" of being "inflated like a balloon, and ready to start," Mr. Bounderby is like a monstrous cartoon. He boasts constantly—as he does here to the helpless Mrs. Gradgrind—of being a "self-made" man, meaning someone who has risen unaided up the social ladder. In a memorable phrase, Dickens calls him the "bully of humility." By this he means that Bounderby uses the squalor and misery of his upbringing—all the stories he tells in this chapter about being born in a ditch and raised as a vagabond—to put other people down, exactly as if he were claiming exalted birth and high connections.

Study Questions

1. Gradgrind is "virtually retired" from what occupation?
2. How does Stone Lodge, Gradgrind's house, resemble its owner?
3. Who is often referred to as "eminently practical"?
4. Which character describes himself as "a young vagabond"?
5. Who says, "Go and be somethingological directly."?
6. Signor Jupe, Sissy Jupe's father, performs in the circus with what animal?
7. Mr. Gradgrind's political ambitions include what?
8. Who asked whom to come peep at the circus?
9. Why does Mr. Bounderby always "throw" on his hat?
10. What is Louisa's reaction to Mr. Bounderby's kiss?

Answers

1. Gradgrind has virtually retired from the "wholesale hardware trade."
2. Stone Lodge resembles its owner in several ways. It is square, regular, "balanced" (six windows on one side and six on the other). It is an "uncompromising fact on the landscape." And its portico (covered porch with columns) looks like Gradgrind's forehead.
3. Thomas Gradgrind is referred to as "eminently practical" by fellow Coketowners. He refers to himself as "eminently practical."
4. Mr. Bounderby, recounting his childhood and youth, calls himself a young vagabond.
5. Mrs. Gradgrind is in the habit of saying this when she wants to dismiss the children to their own pursuits. Dickens remarks that she is "not a scientific character."
6. Signor Jupe performs with a trained dog named Merrylegs.
7. Mr. Gradgrind wants to be elected to Parliament.

8. Mr. Gradgrind assumes that Tom brought his sister to the circus; Louisa says that it was she who asked him to go.

9. Mr. Bounderby "throws" on his hat as if to express that he is "a man who had been far too busily employed in making himself, to acquire any fashion of wearing his hat."

10. Louisa reacts with disgust; she is shown frantically trying to rub the spot on her cheek that Bounderby had kissed with her handkerchief, "until it was burning red."

Suggested Essay Topics

1. Write an analysis of Mr. Gradgrind's exchange with his daughter in Chapter 3.

2. Comment on Mr. Bounderby's physical appearance, gestures, and tone of voice and explain what these convey about his personality.

Chapter 5: The Key-Note
Chapter 6: Sleary's Horsemanship

New Characters:

Mr. E.W.B. Childers: *a horse-rider*

Master Kidderminster: *his son*

Emma Gordon: *a pregnant member of Sleary's Circus*

Summary

Gradgrind and Bounderby walk to Coketown in search of Sissy Jupe's father. He lives in Pod's End, a part of town unfamiliar to them both. They stop and look about themselves. Just then Sissy Jupe herself comes into view, running. She is being pursued by Bitzer, the pale boy in her class. Mr. Gradgrind sends Bitzer on his way with a warning and asks Sissy to conduct them to her father's house.

She leads the way to the Pegasus' Arms, a combination inn and pub (drinking house) where Sleary's troupe are staying. While Sissy looks in vain for her father, who is nowhere to be found at the inn, Gradgrind and Bounderby encounter Mr. E.W.B. Childers and his son, Master Kidderminster, both performers in Sleary's Circus. Childers tells them that Sissy's father, depressed by his failures in the ring, has probably left the circus and abandoned his daughter.

Mr. Sleary, preceded by other members of his troupe, arrives on the scene. He asks Mr. Gradgrind if he intends to do anything for the girl whose father has "morrised" (run away). Against Bounderby's advice, Gradgrind offers to take Sissy into his household, to take charge of her, and educate her according to his system, with the understanding that she cease to communicate with any of her old friends. Sleary tells Sissy (who has just returned, frantic, from searching for her father) that she is free to choose whether to stay with the circus, where she will be apprenticed and treated as a daughter by Emma Gordon, or accept Gradgrind's offer. Weeping, Sissy decides to go with Gradgrind, saying farewell to Sleary and to all her old companions.

Analysis

Roughly half of Chapter 5 is a description of Coketown. Dickens uses unusual metaphors and expressive language to convey the strange, nightmarish realities of the industrial city: the factories with their "interminable serpents of smoke," the steam engines whose pistons drive up and down like "the head of an elephant in a state of melancholy madness." He writes of the monotonous routine of the place, how its people do the same work day after day, how even its buildings have a quality of sameness and appear interchangeable with one another, so that "the jail might have been the infirmary, the infirmary might have been the jail, the town hall might have been either, or both, or anything else, for anything that appeared to the contrary in the graces of their construction."

In a variety of ways the circus people present a contrast to what Dickens writes about Coketown. In the first place, as transient entertainers, they are outsiders to the city. They move, dress, and talk distinctively—they use circus jargon, and Sleary speaks with a pronounced lisp. Indeed their whole purpose in life, which is to entertain, is opposed to the spirit of Coketown. Perhaps most striking is that, unlike Coketown, their society appears to function as a loving, cooperative community—they have, as Dickens puts it, "an untiring readiness to help and pity one another."

Despite the apparent agreement in their outlooks, Mr. Bounderby and Mr. Gradgrind respond differently to the circus people. Mr. Gradgrind changes his plan of action when he learns about Sissy's circumstances, generously deciding to take Sissy into his household. Bounderby, on the other hand, carries on in his usual tactless way—he is particularly insensitive to Sissy—and tries to argue Gradgrind out of his decision.

Study Questions

1. What does Coketown's river run with?

2. Coketown's buildings are made of what material?

3. What does Bitzer tell Gradgrind he was about to help Sissy with before she ran away?

4. What is Sissy carrying when she is stopped by Gradgrind and Bounderby?

5. The picture behind the bar in the Pegasus' Arms is of what animal?

6. Why did Signor Jupe enroll his daughter in Gradgrind's school?

7. What is a "cackler"?

8. The "Wild Horseman of the North American Prairies" refers to which of Sleary's performers?

9. Who is "the diminutive boy with an old face"?

10. What does Mr. Sleary declare he has never done yet in his life and doesn't intend to start?

Answers

1. The river in Coketown runs purple with dye.

2. The buildings in Coketown are red and black—red from the brick, black from the soot of the factory chimneys.

3. Bitzer tells Gradgrind he was only trying to help Sissy with her definitions.

4. Sissy is carrying a jar of "nine oils" used by the circus performers to soothe their muscles.

5. The picture in the bar shows a horse.

6. Signor Jupe enrolled Sissy in Gradgrind's school because he "had always had it in his head" to have her educated.

7. A "cackler," in the jargon of the circus, is a speaker.

8. Mr. Childers is billed as the "Wild Horseman of the North American Prairies."

9. The diminutive boy with the old face is Mr. Childers' son and stage partner, Master Kidderminster.

10. Mr. Sleary declares that he has never yet injured one of his horses, and that he has no intention of injuring any of their riders.

Suggested Essay Topics

1. "People mutht be amuthed, Thquire, thomehow." Discuss how Mr. Sleary's statement might be said to express Dickens' own conviction in *Hard Times*.

2. Compare and contrast Mr. Bounderby and Mr. Gradgrind's attitudes and responses to the circus people.

3. Based on what you now know about Sleary's Horse-Riding and Gradgrind's establishment, explain why you think Sissy was right or wrong in accepting Gradgrind's offer.

Chapter 7: Mrs. Sparsit

New Characters:

Mrs. Sparsit: *Bounderby's housekeeper*

Mr. Sparsit: *the lady's late husband*

Lady Scadgers: *her invalid great aunt*

Summary

On the morning following Mr. Gradgrind and Mr. Bounderby's eventful visit with the circus people, Mrs. Sparsit, an elderly widow who acts as Mr. Bounderby's housekeeper, and who is regarded by him (and by herself) as having once been socially very much his superior, chats with her employer over breakfast. Bounderby tells Mrs. Sparsit about what he calls his friend Gradgrind's "whim," his proposal to take care of Sissy Jupe. Bounderby also mentions his own resolution to take "young Tom," Louisa Gradgrind's brother, under his wing by employing him in his office.

To give Gradgrind time to reconsider his decision, Bounderby has put Sissy, whom he calls the "tumbling-girl," up for the night at his house in Coketown. He appears to be concerned that Sissy would not make a suitable companion for Louisa.

When Gradgrind and Louisa arrive at Bounderby's, Sissy is summoned to meet her benefactor. Not aware of Mrs. Sparsit's importance, Sissy fails to include her in her curtsies. Bounderby makes a speech about Sissy's blunder.

Gradgrind explains to Sissy how he means to have her "strictly educated." As a condition for receiving his care, she must never refer to her past. She must stop reading any of the fairy stories she used to read to her father. After this Gradgrind and Louisa, with Sissy, return to Gradgrind's Stone Lodge.

Analysis

Mrs. Sparsit is a minor character, but since her tendency to overreach herself in service to her employer makes her play an important part in the action, she bears thinking about. (Because Dickens lavishes a lot of care on them, even his minor characters not important to the plot bear thinking about.) The elderly, fine-featured Mrs. Sparsit is highly ladylike in manner and appearance; her speech is elaborate and "refined." Long ago she was what is called "well-connected," that is, her family background gave her a good position in society, and even now she has a "titled" relative, a Lady Scadgers. But Mrs. Sparsit married badly, to a drunkard, much younger than herself, who ran through his fortune and left her without any money, and so she has entered Mr. Bounderby's service.

In this chapter and elsewhere, Bounderby is shown making a great fuss over Mrs. Sparsit. He keeps harping on how splendid and fashionable she and her friends once were. Dickens at one point facetiously compares him to her "Conqueror," and she to his "captive Princess." In a sense that really is how Bounderby seems to think of her: as a prize possession, one that enhances his own position. As Dickens puts it, "Just as it belonged to his boastfulness to depreciate his own extraction, so it belonged to it to exalt Mrs. Sparsit's."

For herself, Mrs. Sparsit is as proud of her family connections and her past as Boundary is of his lack of family. From what Dickens tells us of the Powlers, the name of the ancient family that she likes to let slip into conversations, and of Lady Scadgers, Mrs. Sparsit has little cause to think so much of her connections, past and present. Mrs. Sparsit, in fact, is one of Dickens' many satirical studies of unreasonable family pride.

Study Questions

1. What is Mrs. Sparsit occupied in making for her employer?
2. How much does Mr. Bounderby pay yearly for Mrs. Sparsit's services?
3. Where did the late Mr. Sparsit die, and of what?
4. What has to happen before Tom Gradgrind can start to work for Bounderby?
5. Who speaks "with a kind of social widowhood" upon her?
6. Who is said to have a "moral infection of clap-trap in him"?
7. When does Mr. Gradgrind lower his voice?
8. What is the "oversight" Gradgrind mentions?
9. Which of Mrs. Sparsit's facial features are most pronounced?
10. Who is to be "reclaimed and formed" and in what way?

Answers

1. Mrs. Sparsit is preparing Mr. Bounderby's breakfast tea.
2. Mr. Bounderby gives Mrs. Sparsit 100 pounds a year.
3. Mr. Sparsit died from consuming too much brandy in Calais, France.

4. Tom must finish up his education before coming to work for Bounderby.

5. Mrs. Sparsit is said to speak with an air of "social widowhood."

6. This phrase applies to Mr. Bounderby; Dickens is referring to the way strangers, ordinarily modest, take to boasting about him.

7. Mr. Gradgrind lowers his voice when he talks to Louisa about her reading.

8. Mr. Gradgrind is referring to Sissy's failure to include Mrs. Sparsit in her curtseying.

9. Mrs. Sparsit has a long "Coriolanian" (Roman) nose and "dense black eyebrows."

10. Sissy Jupe is to be reclaimed and formed by the education she will receive at Gradgrind's.

Suggested Essay Topics

1. Mrs. Sparsit and Mr. Bounderby are both in their own ways proud people who pretend to be humble. Explain how and in what ways.

2. Examine Mr. Gradgrind's motives for taking Sissy Jupe into his household in the light of what he tells her at Bounderby's house.

Chapter 8: Never Wonder

Summary

Louisa and Tom sit talking by the fireplace in their study at the close of day. Their unhurried conversation starts and stops, with pauses to gaze into the fire. Tom complains bitterly about his life at Stone Lodge, which he calls a "Jaundiced Jail."

Tom brings up the subject of his going to live with "old Bounderby." Louisa asks him if he really looks forward to working for him. Tom replies that "there's one thing to be said for it, it will

be getting away from home." Louisa repeats this remark, word for word, in a "curious tone." Gazing at the fire, she tells Tom she has been "wondering about you and me, grown up." At this point Mrs. Gradgrind intrudes on the scene, complaining that Tom has been encouraging his sister to wonder, "when he knows that his father has expressly said that she is not to do it."

Analysis

In the phrase "never wonder" Dickens proposes a link between his characterization of the joylessly regulated lives of Coketown's workers and what he has so far described of the bringing up of the Gradgrind children. "Louisa, never wonder," her father once told Louisa when she was younger. The workers of Coketown, those "grown-up babies" (the phrase is meant ironically), are given the same message. They are to "take everything on trust," to "take everything on political economy."

But the program of "never wonder," Dickens believes, faces opposition, whether in Gradgrind's nursery and classroom or in the larger world that industrialism is bringing about. As an example of how people will wonder, he points to the works of fiction that, to Gradgrind's consternation, are the most requested books in Coketown's library: romantic tales and works of fiction that treat human beings and human problems as more than matters of fact and calculation and money in the bank.

Talking with her brother, Louisa can't stop herself from wondering. Her "unmanageable thoughts," like those of many young people, circle uneasily around who she is and what her prospects are. There are hints, in her pauses and in the "curious tone" with which she repeats Tom's words about the advantages of a move to Bounderby's, of her upcoming marriage to the banker.

Louisa's love for Tom is evident throughout this chapter. She is saddened because she cannot be a more amusing companion for him. Tom shows some affection for Louisa but is more preoccupied with his plans for leaving home. The difference in their character is further shown by their conversation about the fire. Tom sees nothing in it; Louisa gazes at it and "wonders."

Study Questions

1. What do you think Dickens means by the opening words of Chapter 8, "Let us strike the key-note again, before pursuing the tune"?

2. How many church denominations compete for the allegiance of Coketown's population?

3. Mr. Gradgrind is said to have "greatly tormented his mind" about what?

4. Who does Tom say hates him and all the family?

5. The "Jaundiced Jail" is Tom's way of referring to what?

6. What does Louisa wish she had learned, so as to be able to "reconcile" Tom to conditions at home?

7. What will be Tom's "revenge" when he goes off to work at Bounderby's?

8. In what way does Tom propose to "smooth" and "manage" Bounderby?

9. What does Tom see in the fire?

10. Mrs. Gradgrind repeats which one of her favorite "cogent remarks" to her children?

Answers

1. By the "key-note," Dickens may mean his educational theme, and by the "tune" how it works itself out in the story of Tom and Louisa Gradgrind. The "key-note" might also refer to his evocation of Coketown.

2. There are 18 churches in Coketown.

3. Mr. Gradgrind worries greatly about what books people take out of Coketown's library.

4. Tom believes that Sissy Jupe hates him and all his family.

5. Tom calls Stone Lodge a "Jaundiced Jail."

6. Louisa says she wished she knew how to play an instrument, or sing, or talk amusingly, as other girls have been taught to do.

7. Tom says he will enjoy himself, go out more, and "see something."

8. Whenever Bounderby says anything he doesn't like to hear, Tom will just mention how his sister would be hurt, and how she expects him (Tom) to be treated gently.

9. Tom sees nothing in the fire, "except that it is a fire...and looks as stupid and blank as everything else looks."

10. Mrs. Gradgrind says she wishes she "had never had a family, and then you would know what it was to do without me!" She says the same thing in Chapter 4.

Suggested Essay Topics

1. Discuss the nature of Tom and Louisa's relationship, basing your remarks on the conversation in this chapter.

2. Discuss Mrs. Gradgrind's attitude toward her children. What kind of a parent is she? Can Louisa or Tom look to her for support? If not, why not?

Chapter 9: Sissy's Progress

Summary

Several months have passed since Sissy Jupe has moved into Stone Lodge. She has not done well at school; caring for Mrs. Gradgrind is hard, and she's had "strong impulses" to run away. But the thought of her father stops her—she still has faith that he will return to her some day, and that he would prefer her to remain where she was. After all, it had been his idea to enroll her in Gradgrind's school in the first place.

Mr. M'Choakumchild cannot give Gradgrind a favorable account of her performance. She is slow with figures; can grasp that the world is round but has no interest in its dimensions; cannot remember historical dates unless "something pitiful happened to be connected therewith"; bursts into tears when she is asked to do practical sums, and so on. Disappointed, Gradgrind nevertheless declares that Sissy must be "kept to it."

One night, Sissy approaches Louisa and tearfully confides her school troubles. Louisa, intrigued by Sissy's "wrong" answers, asks about her past life. Interrupted three times by an impatient Tom, who wants Louisa to come into the drawing room to meet Bounderby, Sissy tells the story of both her parents: about her mother, a dancer who died when Sissy was born, and her barely literate father who had somehow gotten the idea (perhaps from his wife, who was literate) that Sissy should be educated. Louisa asks if her father loved his wife, and why he left Sissy—only for her own good, insists Sissy, and because he had failed in his performances as a clown and felt himself to be a disgrace and no good to her.

Ever since this conversation, Louisa stops what she is doing when Sissy asks if there has been any word about her in the mail and looks "as earnestly as Sissy did" for the reply—which, however, is always the same: no.

Analysis

The hail storm of fact that has broken over Sissy's head every day for months has not altered her. She is still recognizably the same simple-hearted girl who was at a loss to define "horse" in M'Choakumchild's classroom. Gradgrind's project to "form" her anew, if it ever does succeed, has a long way to go.

Sissy's poignant narrative of her past life makes us feel that if Gradgrind's project depends on Sissy's forgetting or shedding her past, it will never succeed. Sissy's past is a part of her. So is the story she tells. For if Gradgrind or M'Choakumchild think in figures, Sissy, one might say, thinks in stories.

Notice how much essential rightness, at least from a humanitarian or Dickensian point of view, there is in Sissy's "mistakes." Take for example what she says when M'Choakumchild asks her what percentage 500 deaths by drowning or shipboard fires would be out of 100,000 taking long sea voyages. Her answer, "Nothing... nothing to the relations and friends of the people who were killed," is a truth about suffering and the meaninglessness of statistics to the bereaved.

When Louisa asks Sissy if her father loved Sissy's mother she is, we are made to feel, thinking of her own situation: of her parents' loveless marriage and of Bounderby, whose attentions to her persist. The increasing selfishness of Tom, who for the sake of a dinner invitation is eager to subject her to those attentions, is thrown into high relief in this chapter.

Study Questions

1. Whispering the "awful word," Sissy divulges that her father is a what?

2. What word always reminds Sissy of stutterings?

3. What "terrible communication" does Sissy make about her mother?

4. What does Sissy remember her father doing when she was "quite a baby"?

5. What is Sissy's reply to Louisa's question about where she lived with her father?

6. Which of the stories Sissy read her father did he seem particularly to enjoy?

7. What was the object of Sissy's father's one outburst of anger?

8. Why does every letter that she sees in Mr. Gradgrind's hand take Sissy's breath away and blind her eyes?

9. "That not unprecedented triumph of calculation which is usually at work on number one" refers to which character?

10. Asked for the first principle of political economy, Sissy's "absurd" answer is what?

Answers

1. Sissy tells Louisa that her father is a clown (in the circus).

2. The word "statistics" always reminds Sissy of stutterings.

3. Sissy's "terrible communication" is that her mother was a dancer.

4. Sissy remembers her father carrying her.

5. Sissy says she traveled about the country, never staying in one place.

6. Sissy's father took particular delight in the *Arabian Nights*.

7. The object of Signor Jupe's anger was his trained dog, Merrylegs.

8. A letter in Gradgrind's hand has this effect on her because she supposes it might be either from her father, or from Mr. Sleary, giving news about her father.

9. The phrase refers to young Tom Gradgrind.

10. Sissy's answer is that the first principle of political economy is "To do unto others as I would that they should do unto me."

Suggested Essay Topics

1. Sissy believes herself to be "O so stupid!" for her answers in class. Actually, they show considerable intelligence of a certain kind. Discuss what kind of intelligence that is, as well as what sort of outlook is revealed by her "mistakes."

2. Discuss Louisa's attitude toward Sissy before and after the conversation recorded in this chapter.

Chapter 10: Stephen Blackpool
Chapter 11: No Way Out
Chapter 12: The Old Woman

New Characters:

Stephen Blackpool: *one of Bounderby's "hands"*

Rachael: *a fellow worker*

Stephen's wife: *an unnamed, drunken, sub-human woman*

Summary

Stephen Blackpool, a weaver in Mr. Bounderby's cotton mill, stands searching for someone in the crowd of women leaving the factory at the end of the day. He's a gray-haired man of 40, who speaks in the broad accents of his native Lancashire. His hard life has made him look much older. Just as he's about to turn away disappointed, he sees a familiar shape ahead of him. It is Rachael, his friend and companion for many years. The two greet each other affectionately, but there is a sadness and a certain constraint in their greeting too. Almost her first words are that they ought not to walk together so often, and he agrees—it might cause people to talk. Stephen sees her home and then walks home himself.

He lives in one of the poorest quarters of Coketown, in a single room above a small shop. He keeps it neat with a few simple pieces of furniture. The room is dark. Entering it with a candle, he stumbles over a body. It is his wife, apparently returned from a drunken binge, who has been sitting in a motionless stupor on the floor of his room. She rises, talks angrily and incoherently and then collapses on the bed. Stephen covers her with a blanket and falls asleep on a chair.

The following morning finds Stephen at his power loom. The noon-bell rings. He rises from his work, exits the mill, and makes his way to Mr. Bounderby's residence, which stands on a hill at some distance from Stephen's usual neighborhood. He gives his name to Bounderby's servant.

Bounderby is at lunch, attended by Mrs. Sparsit. He knows Blackpool to be a reliable employee, with nothing "troublesome against him," and so invites him in. Stephen says he has come for advice. He tells Bounderby about his unhappy 19-year marriage to the woman in his room and of her increasing addiction to drink. He says for the past five years he has taken to paying her to stay away, but that now she has returned. He adds that if it were not for the pity and comfort of "th' best lass living or dead" (he means Rachael), he would have gone mad or killed himself. Blackpool asks what he must do to be "rid of her," remarking that he has read in the papers of people set free to marry again from marriages less unfortunate than his.

Mr. Bounderby assures Blackpool that what he wants is out of the question. Only a tiny minority of extremely wealthy people can take advantage of the laws for divorce. For such as Stephen, his duty is plain: he married for better or for worse, and he must stay married. Blackpool takes his leave, with the observation that affairs in England seem to be all in "a muddle," an expression that, however mild, Bounderby reacts to as if he had been preaching subversion.

On his way back to the factory Blackpool is stopped by an old woman, who questions him closely about the occupant of the house from which he has just emerged. In appearance, she is a simple country woman, who, it turns out, travels to Coketown every year just to catch a glimpse of Mr. Bounderby. Learning from Blackpool that he has worked for 12 years in Bounderby's mill, the old woman seizes his hand and kisses it, saying, "I must kiss the hand...that has worked in this fine factory for 12 years!" Back at work, Blackpool sees the old woman still outside the factory, gazing up at the building, apparently "lost in admiration."

When the evening bell sounds, Blackpool joins the throng leaving the factory and once again looks for Rachael, even though he knows she has warned him against being seen too much together. She is not there. Before returning to the home he now dreads, he stays out late, brooding.

Analysis

Dickens wrote extensively and knowingly about England's poor, including some of the very poorest, and even more about the "shabby genteel" class from which he himself came. But never before *Hard Times* had he written about factory workers. Now and then, in these chapters and others where Stephen Blackpool and Rachael figure, we sense that he is straining to imagine much that is unfamiliar, trying hard to fairly represent a way of life and settings that were fundamentally alien to him.

Blackpool, as will become even more apparent later on in the novel, serves as a mouthpiece for Dickens' own views (as Mr. Sleary and Sissy Jupe do as well). His "tis a' a muddle" is a sentiment, or an observation, on the increasingly problem-ridden character of the civilization that he and Dickens inhabited. Perhaps, then, Bounderby is not so far off the mark to suspect Stephen of disrespect for "the institutions of your country," however preposterous his claim to see in Stephen's "unhallowed opinions" "traces of the turtle soup, and venison, and gold spoon." (In Chapter 11 Dickens writes that Bounderby "always represented...[as] the sole, immediate and direct object of any Hand," to be "set up in a coach and six, and to be fed on turtle soup and venison, with a gold spoon.")

At first glance it might seem surprising that Blackpool would plausibly expose so much of his private anguish and ask his employer for advice about his terrible domestic situation. It makes one wonder if that was the only way Dickens could think to manage Blackpool and Bounderby standing on the same piece of parlor carpet. It is certainly true that, in this novel, only the most melodramatic circumstances seem to bring the working class and middle or upper class characters together.

Study Questions

1. Who are the "Hands" of Coketown?

2. Only in his expression does Blackpool resemble what set of men?

3. What do travelers by express train say about the spectacle of Coketown's factories at night?

4. How old is Rachael?

5. Why does the undertaker in Rachael's neighborhood have a black ladder?

6. The "crashing, smashing, tearing piece of mechanism" refers to what?

7. How does Mrs. Sparsit react when Blackpool says he has come to ask, "How I am to be ridded o' this woman?"

8. How has the old woman traveled to Coketown?

9. How long has Blackpool worked in Gradgrind's factory?

10. Why does Stephen again look for Rachael among the women leaving the factory?

Answers

1. The "Hands" refers to the great majority of Coketown's population, those who work in its factories.

2. Blackpool's face looks intelligent, but he is not one of those workers who, "piecing together their broken intervals of leisure through many years, had mastered difficult sciences."

3. The travelers say the factories look, lit up as they are at night, like "Fairy palaces."

4. Rachael is 35.

5. The undertaker has a black ladder "in order that those who had done their daily groping up and down the narrow stairs might slide out of this working world by the windows."

6. The words refer to Blackpool's power loom. Dickens was aware of the hazards to life and limb presented by such machinery, and his journal, *Household Words*, ran articles deploring the safety records in England's factories.

7. Mrs. Sparsit reacts as if she has received a "moral shock."

8. The old woman has traveled to Coketown from the countryside via the "Parliamentary," at a penny a mile the cheapest way to travel by train. England's Parliament had decreed that one such train should run once every day, on all the important lines.

9. Blackpool, as he tells the old woman, has worked in Bounderby's factory for 12 years; he has worked as a weaver most of his life.

10. Blackpool wants to communicate the news of his wife's reappearance to Rachael.

Suggested Essay Topics

1. Dickens calls Stephen Blackpool a "man of perfect integrity." First, what do you think this means, and, second, how in these chapters does his integrity manifest itself?

2. Discuss the significance of the imagery Dickens uses to describe the Coketown factories, particularly the image of the "Fairy palace."

Chapter 13: Rachael

Summary

Stephen returns to his room and finds Rachael attending his wife, who is in a feverish, semiconscious state from which she is not expected to emerge until the morning. Rachael has changed the woman's clothes, tidied and swept the room, and rigged a sheet around the bed, so Stephen can't see her. On a low table by the bed stand two bottles of medicine, one marked "Poison." The sight of it makes him shiver, which Rachael attributes to his staying out late in the heavy rain and high winds.

At Rachael's urging, Stephen goes to sleep in his chair. He dreams that it is his wedding day and he is standing in church by his bride. During the ceremony, he becomes aware of a great light shining from the words of one of the Ten Commandments by the altar. Then he hears the words sounded out, "as if there were voices in the fiery letters." The scene changes, and he is standing with the clergyman before a vast crowd, all staring at his face. He is on a raised stage. Above him is his power loom, which, as he hears the words of the burial service, changes shape, and he knows he is there to be executed. He feels himself falling...and is returned, still dreaming, to regular life, gloomily convinced that he has been condemned never to see Rachael's face again. He is haunted by a shape: the shape of the bottle with the deadly label. Everything he sees keeps turning into the bottle—the very chimneys of the mills turn into the bottle, with the dire warning wrapped around them. Still dreaming, he finds himself back in his own room, in the chair, with Rachael asleep in another chair. The woman behind the sheet starts to move. As if in a trance he watches her reach for the fatal medicine, pour it into a mug, and bring it to her lips. Just at this moment Rachael wakes up and snatches away the cup. Stephen, too, starts out of his chair, demanding to know if he has been awake or dreaming what has just passed.

Rachael calmly gets rid of the poison and says she has to leave. As she is about to descend the stairs, he asks in a low voice if she's not afraid to leave the woman with him alone. Kneeling down to her, he goes on to confess the dark thoughts he had had about the

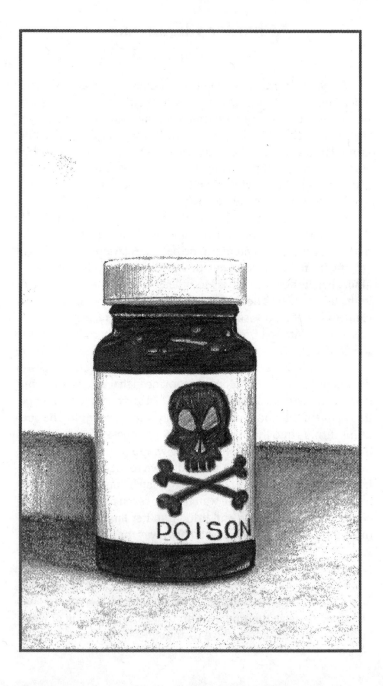

bottle. Horrified, she puts her hands on his mouth. He grasps her hands with his, and, still kneeling, declares that from now on, whenever he sees or thinks of his wife, he will see Rachael beside her as she was this night.

Analysis

Two powerful Victorian stereotypes of women are at play in this chapter. Rachael is the woman as ministering angel, a figure to be worshiped, as Stephen almost literally does at the end of the chapter. The other, his wife, is the woman of abandon with degraded appetites. Dickens has made Stephen's unnamed wife a chronic alcoholic into the bargain, so that there is never any possibility of learning what her perspective might be on her situation. This is because she has no perspective, Dickens evidently not thinking it necessary to endow her with one. She is in fact a creature barely human, a monstrous, deformed thing who must, rather like the "Elephant Man" be kept hidden behind a sheet.

Stephen's wife was once a girlhood friend of Rachael's. Rachael's loyalty to her old friend, and her certainty that Stephen would want her to, made her come to the woman's aid. In a chapter supercharged with Christian imagery, Rachael quotes the words of Jesus: "Let him who is without sin among you cast the first stone at her!"

This chapter, in which at one point all three people slip in and out of conscious awareness, is a good example of Dickens' remarkable pre-Freudian familiarity, not just with the secret and forbidden impulses and wishes revealed in dreams, but with border states between consciousness and unconsciousness.

Study Questions

1. What object makes Stephen compare Rachael to the stars?
2. What item of Rachael's clothing does Stephen kiss?
3. How many times does he kiss it?
4. What does Rachael break on the hearth?
5. Whose little sister is imagined to be among the angels?
6. The red finger marks on Rachael's forehead are from what?

7. Who is the woman Stephen stands beside in church, in the "imaginary happiness" of his dream?

8. Which of the Ten Commandments would it seem Stephen sees and hears in his dream?

9. What time is it when Stephen and Rachael both wake?

10. During the whole of this chapter, what is happening outside Stephen's room?

Answers

1. The candle in his window makes Stephen compare her to the stars. His idea is that Rachael sheds her light down on the ordinary circumstances of his life as the "shining" far-away stars do the "heavy" candle, with its low light.

2. Stephen kisses the fringes of Rachael's shawl.

3. He kisses her shawl twice.

4. After emptying it, Rachael breaks the bottle marked "Poison" on the hearth.

5. Rachael speaks of a younger sister who died. In his final speech to her, Stephen speaks of how they will one day "walk together far awa', beyond the deep gulf, in th' country where thy little sister is."

6. The marks on Rachael's face are from the blow Stephen's wife gives her when Rachael takes away the mug.

7. The woman he dreams he is marrying is neither his wife nor Rachael but another woman "on whom his heart had long been set."

8. The two likeliest possibilities are either the "Thou shalt not kill," or the "Thou shalt not commit adultery," or both at once.

9. It is three in the morning when Rachael and Stephen awaken.

10. All night a storm blows and rain falls outside of Stephen's room.

Suggested Essay Topics

1. Chapter 13 is both sentimental and melodramatic, two quali-
    ties that are found frequently in Dickens' work. First, look
    these words up in the dictionary and explain how the defi-
    nitions apply to the events in the chapter and the way it is
    written. (If you don't think they do, say why not.)

2. State how you think Dickens prepares the way for the cli-
    mactic emotional intensity of the scene between Stephen
    and Rachael in the rest of Chapter 13.

3. Write an interpretation of Stephen's dream, relating the epi-
    sodes in the dream to events in his life. Then suggest how
    Dickens manages to make this dream so "real."

Chapter 14: The Great Manufacturer
Chapter 15: Father and Daughter

Summary

The years pass, bringing change to the inhabitants of Gradgrind's
establishment. Gradgrind has been elected to Parliament, as a member for Coketown. Sissy Jupe, through with school (Gradgrind sees
no point in her continuing; her performance there has been as con-
sistently disappointing as her services to the family have been ap-
preciated), has been asked to stay on at Stone Lodge under
Gradgrind's protection. Tom, as expected, has gone to work for Mr.
Bounderby's bank. He lives with Bounderby now, working hard during the day but enjoying his evenings. If Bounderby comes on too
strong, all he has to do is mention his sister and he softens—which
is just what Tom said would happen, back when Louisa gazed into
the fire, wondering what the future would bring.

Louisa herself, Mr. Gradgrind has to acknowledge, is now really not just "almost a young woman" but "quite a young woman."
They must talk; father and daughter need to have a serious conversation. He asks her to see him in his study after breakfast the
next morning.

The serious conversation takes place as scheduled. Gradgrind

tells Louisa that Bounderby has asked him for her hand in marriage. Bounderby has, he says, "long watched your progress with particular interest and pleasure." Louisa wants to know if her father thinks she loves Mr. Bounderby? Gradgrind says he cannot tell. Does he wish her to love Mr. Bounderby? Her father, at first unsure how to answer, advises her to consider her decision strictly on the basis of Fact. What are the Facts in the case? He's much older than she is, but (particularly when the latest available statistics on marriage are taken into account) that need not be viewed as an obstacle. In every other respect, Gradgrind says, they are suitably matched.

The "only remaining question" then becomes, Gradgrind tells his daughter, "Shall I marry him?" All along Louisa has been looking very searchingly at her father. A moment comes when she might have opened up to him, showing him "the pent-up confidences in her heart." But the moment passes, and Louisa, remarking, "What does it matter?" asks her father to tell Bounderby that "since he likes to take me thus, I am satisfied to accept his proposal."

Mr. Gradgrind and Louisa go to the drawing room, where her mother is lying down, attended by Sissy. Mr. Gradgrind introduces Louisa as "Mrs. Bounderby." Her mother congratulates Louisa and starts worrying what she is going to call her new son-in-law: "Josiah" won't do, "Joe" is out of the question...Sissy, when she hears Mr. Gradgrind's announcement, looks toward Louisa with "a multitude of emotions," in which appear wonder, pity, sorrow, and doubt.

Analysis

Mr. Gradgrind, who has up to now shown more than a few traces of ordinary humanity, in Chapter 15 is shown once more as a fanatic, a man so blindly and willfully devoted to his principles and his system that he fails to perceive his own daughter's true feelings about the proposal of marriage he conveys to her. In a sense, the completeness of his failure can be traced to the "success" of his system as it has worked to form Louisa into the person she is. If Louisa had not been raised in an environment kept purposefully free of all sentiment, her own feelings would not be so hidden from herself and from all others, including her father.

The scene between Louisa and her father has a significance beyond Dickens' objections to Gradgrind's educational philosophy, however. In its depiction of the barriers to communication that can rise up between parent and child, thwarting understanding and love, Dickens has tapped deep into some unhappy truths about human relations across the generations.

It is interesting to think what a Victorian reader would be likely to make of Chapter 15. Nineteenth-century mythology held the authority and wisdom of the father, the paterfamilias, sacred; here is a father whose every word of advice and counsel could not be more grievously mistaken and harmful. For a young woman, as for her parents—especially her mother—marriage was regarded by the Victorians as a uniquely joyous and significant event; but here is Louisa, saying what does it matter, and her mother worrying about what to call her son-in-law.

Chapter 14 is primarily a transitional chapter, intended to register the passing of time, advance the characters and keep the story moving, with no big dramatic scene. But notice the complexity and evocativeness of the extended metaphor giving the chapter its title and its structure: the idea of time as a great manufacturer. The closing sentences, in which Old Time appears as "that greatest and longest-established Spinner of them all," whose factory is "a secret place, and whose Hands are mutes," is particularly suggestive.

Study Questions

1. Of what aspects of Sissy's performance in school does Mr. Gradgrind complain?

2. What does Dickens mean when he writes that Gradgrind has become "one of the respected members for ounce weights and measure, one of the deaf honorable gentlemen, dumb honorable gentlemen, blind honorable gentlemen, dead honorable gentlemen, to every other consideration"?

3. When does Louisa give her father the same look as the night she was found peeping at the circus?

4. When Tom says to his sister, "It would do me a great deal of good if you were to make up your mind to I know what, Loo. It would be a splendid thing for me. It would be uncommonly jolly!" what is he alluding to?

5. Why is Gradgrind's study "quite a blue chamber"?

6. What does Louisa say when her father announces that she has been the subject of a proposal of marriage?

7. Mr. Gradgrind reminds Louisa that much depends on the sense in which a certain expression is used. What is that expression?

8. What is it, in the course of his conversation with his daughter, that Mr. Gradgrind takes satisfaction in knowing?

9. What does Louisa look at for a long time as she considers what to say to her father?

10. What is Louisa's new attitude to Sissy, from the moment she senses her response to her upcoming marriage?

Answers

1. Mr. Gradgrind is "greatly disappointed" by Sissy's deficiency in acquiring facts and her limited acquaintance with figures.

2. Dickens means that Gradgrind has been elected to Parliament, where he is among those who speak for the interests of the manufacturers.

3. Louisa looks at her father this way when he exclaims, "My dear Louisa, you are a woman!"

4. Tom is alluding to his sister marrying Bounderby.

5. The room is blue because Gradgrind collects the famous series of "blue books," so called because of their blue covers, issued by the government and containing statistical information on such matters as population, wages, and working condition in factories and mines. The information in the blue books was used by many different observers and critics to advance many different arguments and come to many different conclusions.

6. Louisa keeps silent when she hears this; her father has to repeat what he has said, and even then she makes no reply other than to say she wishes to hear her father state the proposal to her. Her apparent composure momentarily flusters her father.

7. The expression Gradgrind refers to is "love."

8. Mr. Gradgrind takes satisfaction in knowing that his daughter does not come to the consideration of the question of marriage with any of "the previous habits of mind, and habits of life, that belong to so many young women."

9. Louisa looks out her father's study window at the factory chimneys of Coketown.

10. Louisa becomes from that moment proud, cold, and impassive toward Sissy, "changed to her altogether."

Suggested Essay Topics

1. Examine Dickens' metaphor of time as a manufacturer and compare it to some other example of metaphoric language in *Hard Times*.

2. Write a defense of Louisa's education, or elements of it, in which you show that its outcome could have been very different.

Chapter 16: Husband and Wife

Summary

Mr. Bounderby's first concern, when he hears that Louisa will have him, is what to say to Mrs. Sparsit, his housekeeper. He is worried that she might have a fit, or cry, or pack up and go to her great aunt, Lady Scadgers—Louisa's coming will mean her services in his house will no longer be needed. When he does summon the nerve to tell her, Mrs. Sparsit's reaction is unexpected. She takes it all in stride, as if she'd been expecting the news all along, and her manner toward him changes. She says she wishes he may be happy, but her tone implies that he won't, and that he is very much to be pitied, as a kind of victim. Bounderby, baffled and resentful but not wanting to lose his prize piece of gentility, proposes that, for the same salary, Mrs. Sparsit stay on as a housekeeper for some apartments above his bank, one of which would be for her exclusive use. This offer Mrs. Sparsit gratefully accepts.

A wedding in one of Coketown's churches is planned. Mr. Bounderby, as an "accepted wooer," appears at Stone Lodge, bearing bracelets. The day comes, the couple is married, and they go home to a wedding feast at Stone Lodge. Mr. Bounderby gives a speech of thanks to the assembled guests, very much in the style of all his speeches, on any occasion. He wants his friends to know that he is Josiah Bounderby of Coketown, that marrying Tom Gradgrind's daughter—who, he says, he believes is worthy of him, just as he thinks he is worthy of her—makes him "feel independent," that he never looked to such a thing occurring when he was a ragged little street boy, and that he hopes "every bachelor may find as good a wife as I have from the harness in which a conventional hack [horse for hire] like myself works."

On her way downstairs, dressed for her honeymoon, Louisa encounters her brother. His face is flushed, either from his feelings or from wine. He has been waiting for her. He wants to thank her for being such a game girl, such a first-rate sister.

Analysis

Dickens offers some uncompromising satire on how the parties concerned in this chapter view the holy state of matrimony. Among them love "took a manufacturing aspect. Dresses were made, jewelry was made, cakes and gloves were made, settlements were made, and an extensive assortment of Facts did appropriate honor to the contract. The business was all Facts, from first to last." The note of disgust here is striking, and may reflect (as does Blackpool's trapped frustration) Dickens' own marital turmoil at the time the novel was written.

Part of the fascination, and much of the comedy, of Bounderby's dealings with Mrs. Sparsit, and hers with him, is that they need each other to complete their ideas of themselves. Bounderby needs Mrs. Sparsit to maintain his presentation of himself as a man with no connections who is yet successful enough to retain a lady of great social distinction. Mrs. Sparsit needs Bounderby to reinforce the idea of her own gentility, which as the years pass recedes further and further into the past. What is a little startling about their relationship, revealed in this chapter more openly than before, is that Bounderby and Mrs. Sparsit carry on for all the world like an old married couple.

(Note, for example, Mr. Bounderby's remark, "Don't go to the North Pole, ma'am!" when Mrs. Sparsit draws her chair away from his.) In a sense, then, his upcoming marriage to Louisa will not be his first bad marriage, for all of Bounderby's harping on his bachelorhood; and Sparsit and Bounderby can be seen to take their place among the other unhappy couples in *Hard Times*.

Study Questions

1. The "deadly statistical recorder" in Gradgrind's study refers to what?

2. When is Louisa, for the first time, a little shaken in the reserved composure she adopts on her wedding day?

3. What does Mrs. Sparsit prefer that Mr. Bounderby call the "terms" (salary) of her employment?

4. What sort of factual knowledge do the wedding guests bring to the Gradgrind-Bounderby wedding feast?

5. Mrs. Sparsit says she has long been under the necessity of "eating the bread of dependence"; what in fact is her favorite supper dish?

6. What precaution does Mr. Bounderby take before communicating to Mrs. Sparsit the news of his upcoming marriage?

7. What horrific image does Mrs. Sparsit's operation with a scissors on a piece of cambric suggest to Dickens?

8. Where are Louisa and Bounderby going on their honeymoon, and what does Bounderby look forward to finding out when they get there?

9. Mrs. Sparsit accepts her new position at the bank, after assuring herself of what one thing?

10. Louisa and Bounderby are married in a church with what distinctive architectural feature?

Answers

1. The phrase, part of another extended metaphor, refers to Gradgrind's clock.

2. Louisa's assumed composure is shaken when her brother embraces her at the bottom of the stairs.

3. Mrs. Sparsit prefers the phrase "annual compliment."

4. The guests know what everything they eat and drink is made of, how it was imported or exported, and so forth.

5. Mrs. Sparsit's favorite supper dish is sweetbreads (veal pancreas) in a "savory brown sauce."

6. Mr. Bounderby stops by a chemist's (pharmacy) to pick up a bottle of smelling salts before his conversation with Mrs. Sparsit.

7. Mrs. Sparsit at work picking out holes with a scissors on a piece of cambric suggests the image of a "hawk engaged upon the eyes of a tough little bird."

8. The Bounderbys are traveling to Lyons, in France; Mr. Bounderby wants to look into how the French "hands" are treated, and whether they too "required to be fed with gold spoons."

9. Mrs. Sparsit wishes to make sure that in accepting this new position she is not further descending the social scale (from personal housekeeper).

10. The church in which Louisa and Bounderby are married has "florid wooden legs."

Suggested Essay Topics

1. Supply either Tom or Sissy Jupe (or both) with wedding toasts.

2. Speculate on the motives for Mrs. Sparsit's newfound compassion for her employer.

3. Compare and contrast Mr. Bounderby's speech on his wedding day with any one of his speeches of comparable length.

Hard Times, Book II: Sowing

Chapter 1: Effects in the Bank
Chapter 2: Mr. James Harthouse
Chapter 3: The Whelp

New Character:

Mr. James Harthouse: *a gentleman from London, newly recruited to Gradgrind's party*

Summary

It is the end of a hot summer day in Coketown, some time after Bounderby and Louisa's wedding. Mrs. Sparsit is installed at the bank. Bitzer, Gradgrind's diligent old pupil, now employed at the bank as a porter (and as Bounderby's informant and spy) keeps her company while she consumes a late afternoon tea.

The conversation turns to Louisa's brother Tom, whose presence in the bank Bitzer resents. Bitzer says Tom is a slacker with expensive habits, and that he wouldn't be where he was if he didn't have a "friend at court," meaning his sister, Louisa.

A knock at the door interrupts their chat. Bitzer lets in a well-dressed man of 35 or so, well-spoken, handsome, a gentleman. He explains he is in Coketown to meet Mr. Bounderby, that he carries a letter of introduction to Bounderby from Mr. Gradgrind, and that he has been mistakenly directed to the bank by a passing mill hand. Mrs. Sparsit is only too happy to give him directions to Mr. Bounderby's residence—and to enlighten him about the Bounderby family, especially Louisa.

The strange gentleman is Mr. James Harthouse, a man of good family who has done a little of everything in his time, and been bored by it all. Mr. Bounderby visits Harthouse at the hotel where he is staying, gives him the standard Bounderby version of Coketown, and invites Harthouse home for dinner, where he will be glad to introduce him to "Tom's Gradgrind's daughter." (Bounderby habitually refers to his wife this way.)

Harthouse is duly introduced and finds himself intrigued by her combination of intelligent reserve and self-reliance, as well as the obvious embarrassment she exhibits over her husband's boasting. When Tom enters the room, late for dinner, Harthouse is able to observe what Louisa's face looks like when it softens toward someone she holds dear, and he likes what he sees. Suddenly Harthouse is very glad he has come to Coketown.

After dinner, Tom directs the visitor back to his hotel. When Harthouse invites him up for a smoke, Tom accepts immediately. The confidences about his sister that Harthouse has been looking for are not hard to coax out of the boy. It requires a little direct flattery here, a little indirect flattery there, and more and more drink. Before Tom passes out, he has told his new friend the whole story of Louisa's unfortunate marriage, including his own part in the disaster.

Analysis

The character James Harthouse is in part a study of an outsider, a well-born dilettante and amateur in a world dominated by professionals and parvenus like Bounderby who boast of their lack of family connections. An experienced traveler who seems to have no permanent roots, he views Coketown with the jaundiced eye of a tourist, and the Coketowners as curiosities. His "going in" for the Utilitarianism of the "hard fact men" is, for him, no more than a whim, although his new associates are distinctly pleased by the prospect of backing from a gentleman of his kind and take it seriously. Political power in England in 1854 was still very much con-

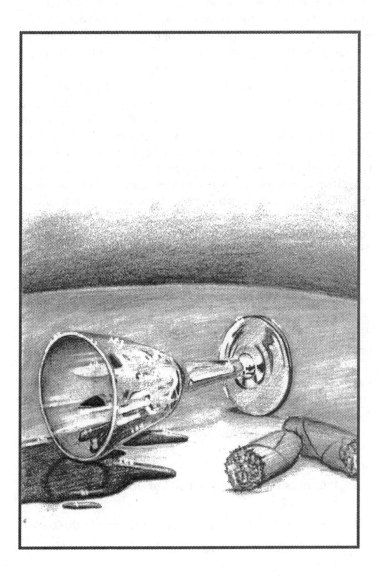

tested between men like Bounderby and Gradgrind and the nonmanufacturing, nonmercantile upper classes whose wealth was in land. Aristocratic endorsement for the dogmas Bounderby and Gradgrind keep repeating would be rare enough to cherish, as Gradgrind and Bounderby do Harthouse.

Mr. Harthouse's chief business in the story will be as a smooth-tongued seducer of Louisa, whose remoteness and evident lack of ease in her surroundings so intrigue him. From his first visit his lazy, humorous talk and correctness of manner make Bounderby look like a boor—not that just about anyone wouldn't. But Louisa is not to be lured by him into cheap shots at her husband. Note the quiet but sharp rebuff she delivers to his somewhat clumsy mockery of Bounderby as "a noble animal in a comparatively natural state": "You respect Mr. Bounderby very much…it is natural that you should." Harthouse immediately feels himself to be "disgracefully thrown out, for a gentleman who has seen so much of the world."

Harthouse is, in his facile way, intelligent—enough so to appreciate Louisa's intelligence, anyway, or to come up with the perfectly apt phrase "the whelp" for her brother. He is in some ways as disgusted with what he sees in Coketown as Dickens. And he's often very funny. Perhaps in order not to let him grow too much in the reader's sympathies, Dickens now and again plants sinister, even supernatural suggestions about the smooth-tongued Harthouse. In Chapter 3, for example, he appears in a distinctly demonic light: he's an "agreeable demon," a "tempter," who has only to "hover" over Tom to take away his soul.

Study Questions

1. Why does Dickens declare that Coketown's very existence is a wonder?

2. What "fiction of Coketown" takes the form of a threat?

3. The Fairy Palaces, on hot days, have the atmosphere of a what?

4. After office hours in Bounderby's bank, what room does Mrs. Sparsit like to sit in?

5. What does Mrs. Sparsit like to think of herself as, and what do people passing by Bounderby's bank think of her as?

6. Bitzer shows himself to be an "excellent young economist" in what remarkable instance?

7. Why does Mrs. Sparsit exclaim, "O you fool!" to herself, after Harthouse has left the bank?

8. In the sentences "They liked fine gentlemen; they pretended that they did not, but they did. They became exhausted in imitation of them..." who is meant by "they"?

9. What does Bounderby tell Harthouse of Coketown's smoke?

10. Before the family dinner, what does Bounderby propose that he and Harthouse do?

Answers

1. Dickens speaks of Coketown in this manner because its leading manufacturers are always claiming to be "ruined."

2. This fiction of Coketown is the manufacturers' talk, whenever they feel their profits are being interfered with, of throwing all their property into the Atlantic.

3. The Fairy Palaces, or factories, have on hot days the atmosphere of a simoon (a desert wind).

4. The room Mrs. Sparsit likes at that hour is a managerial boardroom.

5. Mrs. Sparsit likes to think of herself as the Bank Fairy; passersby see her as the Bank Dragon.

6. Bitzer's excellence as an economist lies in his having consigned his own mother to a workhouse.

7. She is most likely referring either to her employer or to Louisa; to Bounderby, because she senses how unattractive he will seem next to a man like Harthouse; to Louisa, because Mrs. Sparsit assumes she will prove dangerously susceptible to Harthouse's charms.

8. The "they" referred to are the adherents of Gradgrind's philosophy.

9. Bounderby assures Harthouse that the smoke from Coketown's chimneys is "the healthiest thing in the world in all respects, and particularly for the lungs."

10. Bounderby proposes to take Harthouse on a "round of visits to the voting and interesting notabilities of Coketown and its vicinity."

Suggested Essay Topics

1. Macaulay, the great Victorian man of letters and historian, famously dismissed *Hard Times* for what he called its "sullen socialism." Cite evidence to support this observation, in this chapter and elsewhere. If on the contrary you think Dickens is no socialist, sullen or otherwise, explain why.

2. Analyze the interchanges between Louisa and Harthouse for any preliminary hints of her attraction to him.

3. Indicate why you think Tom finds Harthouse so attractive.

Chapter 4: Men and Brothers
Chapter 5: Men and Masters

New Character:

Slackbridge: *trade union leader*

Summary

The union leader Slackbridge holds forth to a large, attentive audience of working men. He has learned of a working man among them who has declined to support certain measures proposed by Coketown's union of factory operatives. Slackbridge, addressing a meeting of The United Aggregate Tribunal, denounces this man as a "traitor and a craven and a recreant." The crowd, which had been with him, is divided—there are calls from the hall to see the man himself and hear what he has to say.

The holdout is Stephen Blackpool, who in refusing to join in with the others is acting out of his own conviction that the union is wrong in its demand for "regulations" in the mills. He is also, as he explains in a short but eloquent speech that contrasts favorably with Slackbridge's overheated verbiage, remaining true to a promise he has made to stay out of trouble (the promise, to Rachael, is alluded to in Chapter 10). The chairman of the meeting pleads with Stephen to reconsider, to "come in" with the others so as to avoid being "sent to Coventry" (ostracized or shunned). Stephen, his mind made up, slowly walks out of the hall.

For the next four days Stephen lives and works in complete isolation. He avoids meeting with Rachael for fear that were she to be seen in his company she too would be punished. One evening, on the fourth day of his ostracism, Blackpool is approached by Bitzer, Bounderby's porter and general spy, to say that Bounderby wishes to have a word with him.

At Bounderby's, in the presence of Louisa, Tom and Harthouse, Stephen is called upon to explain his refusal to join the Coketown "Combination" (union). Bounderby becomes indignant when Stephen persists in defending his fellow workers and speaks again of everything being "all a muddle." The workers, Stephen maintains, keeping his eyes on Louisa's face, don't need the "strong hand," or being told they are always in the wrong, or treated as so many machines. As Stephen turns to go, Bounderby, thoroughly exasperated, fires him on the spot.

Analysis

Blackpool has now been rejected both by his fellow workers and his employer. His isolation is therefore complete, and his future in Coketown looks hopeless. His speeches in these two chapters, particularly at Bounderby's, come as close as any in the novel to representing Dickens' own views, down to Dickens' insistence that industrialism neglects the imaginative side of human existence: it will never do, Stephen says, to "regulate" workers as if they were machines, "wi'out memories and inclinations, wi'out souls to weary and souls to hope."

Dickens places in Blackpool's mouth his own belief that workers were wrong to organize themselves into trade unions. It is difficult to see how else the conditions that Dickens elsewhere deplores could be changed other than by collective action. But

Dickens, who was first and last an individualist, clearly had little or no faith in such action. Finding a way out of the "muddle," he has Stephen say, should not be up to him but to those who have been placed over him. The belief that England's social ills were the responsibility of its rulers was one Dickens held to all his life.

In his depiction of Slackbridge, Dickens shows his contempt for rabble-rousing orators. He contrasts Slackbridge with his audience, very much to the audience's favor: he was "not so honest, he was not so manly, he was not so good-humoured; he substituted cunning for their simplicity, and passion for their safe, solid sense." Slackbridge's oratorical style, with its biblical allusions and references to "glorious rights of Humanity," "holy and eternal privileges of Brotherhood" resembles that of overly pious preachers, a type Dickens particularly disliked and made fun of in many novels.

Study Questions

1. What does Dickens find notably lacking in the meeting of the Coketown workers?

2. The man who, in Slackbridge's speech, "deserts his post, and sells his flag," refers to whom?

3. A "strong voice" in the meeting hall calls for what?

4. Blackpool makes no complaint about being made into an outcast but asks that he be allowed just one thing. What thing is that?

5. Who during the meeting feels "more sorry than indignant" toward Blackpool?

6. What does Slackbridge, acting like "fugleman" (a drill sergeant) call for as soon as Stephen leaves the meeting hall?

7. What are Mr. Bounderby's first words to Stephen, and why do they fall "rudely and discordantly" on his ears?

8. About what does Stephen say he is as sorry as Bounderby?

9. How does Stephen manage to most exasperate Bounderby?

10. Why does Stephen object to Bounderby's talk of imprisoning Slackbridge and other leaders like him?

Answers

1. Dickens points out that the audience betrays no sign of "carelessness, no languor, no idle curiosity."

2. Slackbridge uses these words to refer to Stephen Blackpool.

3. The strong voice demands that if Blackpool is present he be heard from.

4. Stephen asks that he be allowed to remain working.

5. Most of the audience feels this way toward Stephen.

6. Slackbridge calls for "three cheers" for the union after Stephen leaves the hall.

7. Bounderby's first words to Stephen are to "speak up"; they fall rudely and discordantly on his ears because they "seemed to assume that he really was the self-interested deserter that he had been called."

8. Stephen says he is as sorry as Bounderby is when the people's leaders are bad.

9. Without being conscious of it, Bounderby is particularly exasperated that Stephen addresses all his words to Louisa.

10. Stephen thinks that the trouble does not lie with the leaders and thus will not be removed even if they are.

Suggested Essay Topics

1. Discuss Dickens' attitude toward the audience in the meeting hall in the light of his apparent opposition to unions.

2. Discuss the attitude, or combination of attitudes, displayed by Stephen Blackpool during his second visit to Mr. Bounderby's.

Chapter 6: Fading Away

Summary

Stephen, Rachael, and the mysterious old lady, who has reappeared outside Bounderby's house and has been hospitably invited
for tea in Stephen's room, are just about to settle down to their meal
when Stephen's landlady comes up the stairs and whispers the
name of some visitors in Stephen's ear. Catching the name
Bounderby, the old lady retreats fearfully into a dim corner of the
room. Stephen, candle in hand, shows Louisa up. She is followed
by her brother, Tom. She has come, Louisa tells Stephen, because
of what has just happened at her husband's. She wants to know
what plans he has, and if there is really no hope of his finding work
in Coketown. Louisa then offers him money; Stephen, declining
the much larger amount she produces from her purse, thankfully
agrees to accept two pounds from her.

Tom, who has not been paying much attention to any of this,
beckons Stephen out of the room and hurriedly explains that he has
thought of a way to do him a good turn. He asks Stephen to "just
hang about the bank an hour or so" for the next few nights until he
leaves Coketown. If Tom can perform this service, he will pass him
the word through Bitzer, the bank porter. Making sure that Stephen
understands what he is to do, Tom rushes off with his sister.

For the next few nights before his departure from Coketown,
Stephen dutifully loiters outside Bounderby's bank, but no mes-
sage comes. Having said his farewells to Rachael, he leaves
Coketown on foot.

Analysis

Dickens heralds Louisa's unexpected appearance in Stephen's
lodgings with the words "For the first time in her life Louisa had
come into one of the dwellings of the Coketown Hands; for the first
time in her life she was face to face with anything like individuality
in connexion with them." The point Dickens is making is that nor-
mally no thought of the Coketown workers as individuals would
ever have occurred to her. She has been brought up to think of
them, not as persons, but as a "something": "something to be

worked so much and paid so much, and there ended; something to be infallibly settled by laws of supply and demand." The episode of Louisa's visit effectively conveys a sense of the extent to which England had become, in the famous phrase of the time, "two nations," each unknown to the other, separated by barriers that could be crossed only by extraordinary initiatives of goodwill.

Study Questions

1. How does the strange old woman come to be in Rachael's company?

2. What do Stephen, Rachael, and the old woman have for their tea, and how does the meal fulfill the standard testimony of the Coketown magnates that "these people lived like princes, Sir"?

3. What name does the old lady give herself and what does she say about her son?

4. Early on in her visit, what potentially hurtful question does Louisa ask Stephen?

5. Louisa learns that her husband's firing of Stephen will have what effect upon Stephen's reputation?

6. What does Dickens say about the manner in which Stephen accepts Louisa's offer of help?

7. What nervous action does Tom perform as he makes his proposal to Stephen?

8. Where do Rachael and Stephen take the old lady shortly after the visitors leave?

9. What feeling comes over Stephen as he waits outside Bounderby's bank?

10. What time of day is it when Stephen leaves Coketown?

Answers

1. The old lady is in Coketown on her mysterious annual pilgrimage. Coming across Rachael on the street outside Bounderby's home, she falls to talking with her—much as once before she had done with Stephen.

2. The tea they consume consists of real tea, lump sugar, a new loaf of bread from a nearby shop, and fresh butter. Dickens suggests that the Coketown magnates would point to these items as evidence of the well-being, or perhaps the profligacy, of their employees.

3. The old lady says her name is Mrs. Pegler and that the son she once had she has since lost. (Stephen and Rachael assume she means he is dead.)

4. Louisa asks Stephen if Rachael is his wife.

5. Louisa learns that, once fired by one employer, Stephen will become known to all the others as a "troublesome," and presumably unemployable, man.

6. Dickens observes that Stephen's acceptance of Louisa's gift had a "grace in it that Lord Chesterfield could not have taught his son in a century." Chesterfield, the eighteenth-century author of *Letters to his Son*, was a frequent target of Dickens' satire.

7. Tom twists and screws his finger in a buttonhole of Stephen's coat.

8. Stephen and Rachael accompany the old lady to the Traveler's Coffee House, an inn near the railway station where she will stay before returning to the country by next morning's train.

9. Outside the bank, Stephen has an uncomfortable sensation of "being for the first time a disreputable character."

10. Stephen leaves Coketown at dawn.

Suggested Essay Topics

1. Discuss what quality of her character is disclosed in Louisa's scene with Stephen.

2. Examine how Dickens lends poignancy to Stephen's early morning departure from Coketown.

Chapter 7: Gunpowder
Chapter 8: Explosion

Summary

Ever since being dazzled, on the evening he first met Louisa, by the affectionate smile she gave to her brother, James Harthouse has wanted the same smile turned on him. His conversion to Bounderby and Gradgrind's political and economic views, his making himself an intimate of the Bounderby household, his becoming a frequent guest at Mr. Bounderby's newly acquired summer house—all have had this same end in view.

Mr. Harthouse knows from Tom's indiscretions the night he got the boy drunk that his sister has entered a loveless marriage for his sake. He also senses that if he appears to take an interest in Tom he will gain her confidence. Accordingly, when Harthouse finds Louisa alone in her favorite spot on the grounds of Bounderby's estate, a secluded clearing in the woods, it is of her brother, and of her brother's problems, chiefly his habit of gambling, that he speaks.

When Tom himself appears through the trees, Harthouse draws him aside for a private talk. Strolling with Tom through Mr. Bounderby's rose garden, Harthouse offers to settle his gambling debts, asking in return only that he act more kindly toward his sister. Tom seems extraordinarily moody and distracted—he keeps tearing up rosebuds, scattering their petals, even chewing the buds. Harthouse's offer to "be his banker," intended to set his mind at ease, has the opposite effect. Apparently, no amount of money from Harthouse would be of any help now.

The following evening, pleased with his progress in gaining Louisa's confidence, Mr. Harthouse is riding back from a public meeting when Bounderby suddenly bursts into view, shouting that his bank has been robbed. It seems a small safe in which Tom routinely locked up the petty cash has been broken into, and about 150 pounds taken. Bounderby suspects Blackpool—he was observed by Mrs. Sparsit and Bitzer loitering outside the bank for several nights in a suspicious manner—and several others, including an old woman known to have been in Blackpool's company.

Mr. Bounderby has come from the bank with Bitzer and a nervous Mrs. Sparsit. He invites Mrs. Sparsit to stay on at his country
house so that she can recover from the shock of the robbery. Tom
is still at the bank, busy with the police. Louisa, terribly worried
about him and what he might have had to do with the robbery,
waits up for his return.

It is after midnight when Tom returns. Dressed only in a loose
robe, Louisa steals into his room, where he lies on his bed pretend-
ing to be asleep. She asks him—begs him, really—if he has anything special to tell her, and "taking him to her bosom as if he were
a child," assures him she will save him no matter what he might
have done. Tom protests that he has nothing to say and keeps telling her to go to bed. Louisa asks him if she should mention their
having been to see the suspected man, Stephen Blackpool. Saying
that it's up to her, Tom gives her a false explanation of what he had
said to Stephen that night and again urges her to go to bed. When
she leaves, he gets up, locks the door, throws himself on his pillow,
and gives way to a flood of tears.

Analysis

Mr. Bounderby's reaction to the bank robbery, his absurd need
to magnify the crime, is at first merely laughable, like so much of
what he says and does. But then his readiness to assign blame and
convict the wrong-doers ahead of time suddenly makes him seem
not simply ludicrous or vulgar—the usual impression given by his
bluster—but actually dangerous, both capable of and prone to acts
of real injustice. Although he is less positive, Mr. Harthouse is
shown to share in the prejudice underlying the automatic assump-
tion that a worker is to blame.

To the existing number of "philosophers" in *Hard Times*, we
must now add James Harthouse. For all his newfound interest in
Utilitarianism, Harthouse doesn't really believe in anything. He
thinks everyone is a hypocrite, that all opinions are hollow (including his own). His favorite motto, "whatever will be, will be" sums
up his essentially detached, planless outlook on life. The
"Harthouse philosophy," Dickens believes, makes him peculiarly
attractive to Louisa. Apart from the obvious advantages that he
possesses over her husband—relative youth, charm of manner—

advantages that make her vulnerable to his amorous advances, his essential nihilism sounds an answering chord in her. It was Louisa, after all, who had replied "what does it matter?" when her father proposed her husband.

The scene between Louisa and her brother that closes Chapter 8, however, might well make the reader wonder whether Mr. Harthouse could ever hope to compete with Tom for Louisa's love. Louisa's appeal to Tom is so passionate that it goes beyond ordinary sisterly affection; the scene has an excited, incestuous quality which is hinted at in Louisa's state of undress, the lateness of the hour, and the quasi-maternal embrace she gives Tom. Louisa's absorption in her brother can be better understood when we consider that the emotional side of Louisa's nature, starved and stunted under Gradgrind, has all her life been entirely wrapped around her brother.

Study Questions

1. According to Mr. Harthouse, what is the only difference between the "hard Fact fellows" and their opponents, the "philanthropists" and "professors of virtue"?

2. What does Mr. Harthouse write to his brother soon after his arrival in Coketown?

3. What does Mr. Bounderby say were the only pictures in his possession as a youth?

4. Who is the previous owner of Bounderby's summer house?

5. In the course of their conversation in the forest clearing, Louisa confides to Harthouse that she has been doing what for her brother, Tom?

6. What is Tom doing as he walks through the trees on Bounderby's estate, not knowing that Harthouse and his sister are observing him?

7. According to Mr. Bounderby, what does Louisa do when she hears the news of the robbery?

8. In discussing who the perpetrators of the bank robbery might be, which of the many "fictions of Coketown" does Mr. Bounderby give voice to?

9. What remains Mrs. Sparsit's "greatest point, first and last"?

10. What does Louisa say she wants to know, when she goes to her brother's room?

Answers

1. Harthouse says the only difference between them is that while the advocates of the hard Fact school and their opponents both know that humanitarianism is "meaningless," their opponents will never say so.

2. Mr. Harthouse writes that the "Bounderbys were 'great fun';...that the female Bounderby...was young and remarkably pretty."

3. In his youth, the only pictures Bounderby ever owned were engravings on the labels for bottles of shoe polish.

4. The previous owner of Bounderby's summer house, one Nickits, is a Coketown industrialist who went bankrupt.

5. Louisa tells Harthouse she has been giving Tom sums of money to cover his gambling debts.

6. Tom is idly beating the branches and scratching the moss off of the trees with his cane.

7. Mr. Bounderby reports to Harthouse that Louisa fainted— "dropped, Sir, as if she was shot when I told her!"—when she hears about the robbery.

8. The "fiction of Coketown" that Bounderby repeats is "Show me a dissatisfied Hand, and I'll show you a man that's fit for anything bad, I don't care what it is."

9. Mrs. Sparsit persists in making a great show of her pity for Mr. Bounderby.

10. Louisa asks Tom if there is some hidden truth that he has to tell her.

Suggested Essay Topics

1. Analyze Bounderby and Harthouse's reaction to the news of the bank robbery, indicating what it reveals of their characters and outlooks.

2. Suggest what light Tom's destruction of the rosebuds in Bounderby's garden sheds on his character.

3. Compare and contrast Dickens' extended description of Bounderby's summer house with his description of Gradgrind's Stone Lodge.

4. Write a paper exploring indications of the intensity of Louisa's feelings for Tom in any of their previous scenes together.

Chapter 9: Hearing the Last of It

Summary

Mrs. Sparsit, invited to stay on at Bounderby's country retreat "to recover the tone of her nerves," settles in to her old role as housekeeper and her new, self-appointed, role as spy. She reclaims her place at Bounderby's table and prowls around the house, keeping her sharp eyes on its inhabitants.

A hastily written note arrives from Stone Lodge, carried by Bitzer, informing Louisa that her mother is seriously ill. Louisa immediately travels to her old home to be at her mother's side. She finds her mother as usual propped up on a couch, with Sissy as ever in attendance. Jane, Louisa's sister, now a girl of 11, is also in the room.

Mrs. Gradgrind is so weak, and she is so wrapped in shawls, that her voice sounds as if it were coming from the bottom of a well. Her mind, never very consecutive, wanders into odd corners. When her eldest daughter is announced, she reverts to the puzzle that confronted her when Louisa's marriage to Bounderby was announced: what name to call her son-in-law. Mrs. Gradgrind asks for Jane to be brought forward, so that Louisa can see how much she is beginning to resemble her older sister.

The resemblance of Jane and Louisa reminds her mother of something she had wanted to speak to Louisa about. Evidently it is something she wants only Louisa to hear, as she asks Sissy to leave the room. She says that Louisa and her brother learned a lot, studying their "Ologies." But that there was something, "not an

Ology at all," that their father missed or had forgotton. What was it? She asks for a pen, to write to her husband and ask him what it might be. Just then, scribbling "figures of wonderful no-meaning" with an imaginary pen, she dies.

Analysis

What Mrs. Sparsit's sharp eyes search out—the intimacy Harthouse is establishing with Louisa, the indifference of Louisa to her husband's comfort or views—confirms her in the poor opinion that she had always held of Bounderby's marriage. Fundamentally, she has lost whatever respect she may have once had for her employer. Her new attitude can be seen in her habit of openly pitying, and secretly scorning, Mr. Bounderby, as she does when she shakes her fist at his portrait.

Mrs. Gradgrind's character has been the least significant, perhaps, of all the characters in the novel, certainly never present for Louisa as a daughter might hope her mother would be. She has been hardly present for anyone, including the reader, except as the source of inane remarks. And yet her death scene is unexpectedly moving. The reader seems to see her for the first time, to become aware of her as a real person who can think, as the weird brilliance of her remark "I think there's a pain somewhere in the room...but I couldn't positively say that I have got it" or her dying half-perception that her husband, for all his "Ologies," has forgotten, or missed, something. In the final phrases of Chapter 9—"and even Mrs. Gradgrind, emerged from the shadow in which man walketh and disquieteth himself in vain, took upon her the dread solemnity of the sages and patriarchs"—Dickens even manages to lend her a quality of *grandeur*, the last word a reader would have thought to connect with her character.

The extraordinary power of the scene owes something to Dickens' psychological acuteness, his alertness to the currents of feeling within the characters, and to the quiet, understated, dispassionate realism of its presentation. Outside of Tolstoy, there is perhaps no more unsentimental deathbed scene in fiction.

Study Questions

1. What is Mrs. Sparsit always smoothing?

2. "Serve you right, you Noodle, and I am glad of it" is said by what character, and what does it mean?

3. The train to and from Bounderby's country retreat passes over what kind of countryside?

4. Why does Dickens speak of Bitzer as a "fit servitor" at death's door?

5. What "idol" has presided grimly over Louisa's childhood?

6. Where is Mr. Gradgrind while his wife lies dying?

7. To whom has Louisa "never softened" since leaving home?

8. With what kind of feeling does Louisa go to see her mother?

9. With what "strange speech" does Mrs. Gradgrind answer her daughter's question as to whether she is in pain?

10. About what does Louisa experience a "rising feeling of resentment" as she stands by her mother's deathbed?

Answers

1. Mrs. Sparsit is always smoothing her mittens.

2. Mrs. Sparsit says this, addressing Mr. Bounderby's portrait; she means, presumably, that the imminent collapse of his marriage will serve him right.

3. The train passes over a "wild country of past and present coal-pits."

4. The extreme pallor of Bitzer's skin is here associated with death.

5. The idol of Reason has dominated Louisa's childhood.

6. Mr. Gradgrind is "hard at it in the national dust-yard," i.e., he is away attending sessions of Parliament.

7. Louisa has never softened to Sissy since leaving home.

8. Louisa goes to see her mother with "a heavy, hardened kind of sorrow upon her."

9. Mrs. Gradgrind answers that "I think there's a pain somewhere in the room...but I couldn't positively say that I have got it."

10. Louisa resents the influence of Sissy on her younger sister.

Suggested Essay Topics

1. Show how Mrs. Gradgrind's deathbed scene, in particular the question Mrs. Gradgrind wants to ask her husband, relates to the larger themes of the novel.

2. Compare and contrast Mrs. Sparsit's attitude to Mr. Bounderby before and after his marriage to Louisa.

Chapter 10: Mrs. Sparsit's Staircase
Chapter 11: Lower and Lower
Chapter 12: Down

Summary

The first chance Mrs. Sparsit gets to spy on Louisa and Mr. Harthouse at Bounderby's country place, she can only watch them— watch them sit close together in the garden one evening, bending toward one another, their heads almost touching—but she can't hear a word. They are talking about Blackpool, and whether he can be responsible for the robbery. Louisa is ready to give him the benefit of the doubt, but she acknowledges how little she knows about him or about any of the men and women of his class. Harthouse comes close to convincing her about Blackpool's probable guilt, and they stroll off for a walk, followed all the while by Mrs. Sparsit's eagle eye.

Back at the bank, with Bounderby away on business for a few days, Mrs. Sparsit keeps alert for any suspicious sign of progress in Mr. Harthouse's campaign of seduction. Having learned from Tom that Harthouse plans to spend the evening with him in Coketown before going away for a while, Mrs. Sparsit leaps to the conclusion that Mr. Harthouse is putting Tom off, and that he is at that very moment with Tom's sister. Impulsively, she hurries onto the train to Bounderby's house in the country. She creeps through the woods and, hiding behind a tree, hears and sees Harthouse, who has himself arrived secretly and on horseback, profess his love many times and place his arm around Louisa's waist.

Mr. Harthouse then rides away, leaving Louisa standing there in the woods, under the driving rain of a thunderstorm. Mrs. Sparsit, prevented by the storm and her own excitement from dis-

covering how Louisa has responded to Harthouse's outpourings, follows her back to the house, waits outside, and is beside herself with triumph when she sees Louisa leave the house, apparently on her way to elope. The now thoroughly rain-soaked, bedraggled housekeeper follows her back to Coketown by train but loses her at the station.

Louisa has gone straight to Stone Lodge, where her father, at home for the Parliamentary vacation, sits working in his study. She appears at his door, wet from the rain, and, sinking into a chair, asks her astonished father if he has trained her from her infancy. To his reply that, yes, he had, she announces that she "curses the hour I was born to such a destiny."

Reminding him of their last long talk, when he had urged the marriage to Bounderby despite her obvious dislike of the man and unpreparedness for such a step, Louisa demands to know whether, had he any way of knowing then that there lingered in her breast "sensibilities, affections, weaknesses capable of being cherished into strength," he would have allowed her to marry? More devastating questions follow, and her father, completely overcome by his daughter's urgency and despair, is reduced to murmuring one-word replies.

Then at last Louisa tells him what she has come to say—that her heart, left uninstructed for years by anything in his teachings, has been stirred by another man. That she may indeed love him. That this man waits for her now—to tell him she would leave with him was the only way to get him to leave her alone. She does not feel sorry or ashamed or degraded; she only knows that nothing in Gradgrind's philosophy can save her. She calls upon her father, now that he has brought her to where she is, to save her in some other way. And then she faints, falling at his feet.

Analysis

These last chapters of the second book show Dickens' mastery of suspense, humor, and dramatic encounter. The suspense is provided by Mrs. Sparsit's metaphor (carried over in the chapter titles) of the staircase down which she sees Louisa descending and by her determined sleuthing and tracking down of the lovers. The occasion for humor is provided by Mrs. Sparsit's almost lunatic eagerness and willingness to ruin her bonnet with standing in the rain, and her clothes by creeping through the forest, so that she comes to present an almost surreal appearance of "stagnant verdure on her general exterior, such as accumulates on an old park fence in a mouldy lane." In Louisa's superb confrontation with her father, Dickens draws on his feeling for the theater. Down to her fainting away, Louisa is transformed in these pages from a reserved, intelligent young woman who rarely shows her feelings to a passionate heroine in a melodrama.

Mr. Gradgrind's part in that melodrama, we gather from Louisa's speeches, has been that of one who has profoundly failed his obligations—who is as guilty as she is for the events that have brought her to him. Only she doesn't feel guilty. But this too her father is answerable for—it is he who with his blind insistence on the cultivation of reason at the expense of affections has deprived her of any normal capacity to feel.

Louisa says she is not reproaching her father, but it is hard to see how else he could understand her. Throughout, Mr. Gradgrind exhibits no resistance to Louisa, none of the iron certainty in the rightness of his way that he has displayed in the past. He seems genuinely overcome, at a loss for words to respond to what his daughter tells him, and (despite what she says) is charging him with.

Study Questions

1. Since when does Mrs. Sparsit complain of her nerves?

2. How does Harthouse describe Blackpool's speech before Bounderby?

3. From the "House of Commons to the House of Corrections," observes Mr. Harthouse, "there is a general profession of morality," with, however, one exception. Which one is that?

4. The expression the "national cinder-heap" refers to what?

5. What rather odd piece of advice does Mrs. Sparsit give her employer?

6. In his study at Stone Lodge, Gradgrind is at work, "proving something." What does Dickens suppose he is trying to prove?

7. When he hears a particularly loud clap of thunder from the storm that has been raging all night, Gradgrind glances toward where?

8. What significant gesture accompanies Louisa's passionate speech to her father?

9. What does Louisa say it would have been better for her to be?

10. Why does Louisa say she was not "wholly indifferent" to the prospect of her marriage to Bounderby?

Answers

1. Mrs. Sparsit's nerves have been in a delicate state ever since the robbery.

2. Mr. Harthouse contemptuously refers to Blackpool's speech as "lengthy and prosy in the extreme...in the humble-virtue style of eloquence."

3. Mr. Harthouse says that the one exception to the professions of morality coming from every side is to be found "among our people"; that is, the "hard fact men," Utilitarians and political economists like her father and his ally Bounderby.

4. "The national-cinder heap" is what Dickens calls Parliament meeting in session, with its members looking for odds and ends in the dust and throwing quantities of that same dust in each other's eyes.

5. Mrs. Sparsit urges Mr. Bounderby to "Be buoyant, Sir!"

6. Dickens has Mr. Gradgrind hard at work, proving that "the Good Samaritan was a Bad Economist."

7. Gradgrind glances toward Coketown, thinking that its tall chimneys might be in danger from the lightning. (That there are living people abroad in the storm, among them his daughter, does not enter his thoughts.)

8. Louisa beats her breasts with both hands.

9. Louisa says it would have been better to have been born stone blind than raised as she has been by her father—at least then, forced to recognize the world's shape through touch, her imagination would have had some practice.

10. Louisa says she had hoped by marrying Bounderby to be "pleasant and useful" to her brother, "the subject of all the little tenderness in my life."

Suggested Essay Topics

1. Explain why you think Dickens tells so much of the action of Chapters 10 and 11 through the eyes of Mrs. Sparsit.

2. Compose a stern reply to Louisa's speech in Chapter 12, in the style of Gradgrind's first appearances in the novel.

3. Discuss the role the weather, particularly the frequent storms, seems to play in *Hard Times*.

Hard Times, Book III: Garnering

Chapter 1: Another Thing Needful
Chapter 2: Very Ridiculous

Summary

Louisa wakens from a deep sleep. She is in her old room, on her own bed. She feels weak and her head hurts. Her little sister Jane is present. Jane tells Louisa that it was Sissy who had prepared the room and brought her there. Louisa turns her head away; just at this moment, she doesn't want to hear about Sissy's kindness and thoughtfulness.

Louisa's father enters the room and sits down beside her. He speaks to her awhile in uncharacteristically subdued tones, holds her hand, gently rearranges her disordered hair, and then when Louisa no longer replies to his questions quietly leaves the room. His place is soon taken by Sissy Jupe, whose steadfast love and loyalty so overwhelm Louisa that she kneels before the girl and asks for her pity and her compassion.

The evening of the day following Louisa's flight to her father's finds Harthouse at his hotel, baffled as to why he has received no word from her. After leaving her on horseback, he had waited up for her all the night, searched for her the whole of the following day, and is now in a state of painful suspense, just settling in to try to read the newspapers when a waiter comes to tell him that a young lady wishes to see him. It is Sissy Jupe, a young woman he has never seen before, come to tell him that he must never see Louisa again as long as he lives, that he must leave Coketown immediately, and that he must never return.

Quietly but implacably, Sissy answers all of Mr. Harthouse's objections, convincing him that to leave and not ever come back is the only honorable course he can take. Saying that he supposed never was a man "placed in a more ridiculous position," Mr. Harthouse agrees to abide by Sissy's wishes. He writes his brother a brief note telling him that he has decided to go to Egypt to explore the Nile, writes letters to Bounderby and Gradgrind to tell them of his departure and where he may be found for the next 10 days, and, almost as soon as the ink is dry on the addresses, leaves Coketown by the next train.

Analysis

Since hearing Louisa's revelations, Thomas Gradgrind seems greatly altered. The first chapter of the third book shows Gradgrind entering into his redemption, a man full of remorse and self-reproach, slow and hesitating in his speech, thoughtful, uncertain, but capable of love and concern.

Mr. Harthouse's surrender to Sissy, who addresses him with speeches that are among the most unrealistic and contrived in the novel, is less surprising than it might be because Dickens has previously placed so much emphasis on the absence in Harthouse of "any earnest wickedness of purpose." (This phrase is found at the beginning of Chapter 8 of the second book.) His only show of resistance comes when, astonished and taken aback by Sissy's declarations, he demands to know whether she has any commission from Louisa. Sissy's reply, that her only commission is her love and trust in Louisa and Louisa's love and trust in her, is said with such persuasiveness and with such a shaming application to Harthouse's abuse of that trust and love, as to be unanswerable. (A Victorian readership would have no difficulty in seeing Harthouse's attempted elopement as an instance of very grave betrayal.)

Study Questions

1. The title of Chapter 1 refers back to which other chapter title, and why?

2. At first Louisa has an impression that all the events of her life since leaving her childhood room are like what?

3. What does Louisa allow her sister to do?

4. What kind of look does Louisa's father have on his face?

5. What does Gradgrind say about himself with special earnestness, and that Dickens gives him credit for believing?

6. What is the belief that Mr. Gradgrind says he has never shared but that now he must consider afresh?

7. Why does Harthouse keep ringing his bell all night for the hotel porter?

8. Where does Harthouse look for Louisa?

9. Why does Harthouse, telling himself that "it may be as well to be in training," order a steak dinner?

10. Of what does Harthouse admit to having taken advantage?

Answers

1. The title of Book 3, Chapter 1 refers to the novel's first chapter, "The One Thing Needful"; the facts that Mr. Gradgrind had there extolled as the one thing needful will not serve now. The "other thing" may be the compassion that Louisa receives from both her father and Sissy.

2. Louisa has the impression that since her wedding, the events of her life are as the shadows of a dream.

3. Louisa allows her sister to hold her hand.

4. Mr. Gradgrind carries a "jaded, anxious look upon him."

5. Mr. Gradgrind insists that he has always meant well by his system.

6. The belief Mr. Gradgrind mentions is that "there is a wisdom of the Heart, and that there is a wisdom of the Head."

7.   He rings for the porter to find out if Louisa has left any messages for him.

8.   He looks for her first at Bounderby's country house and then at his bank, where Tom cannot tell him her whereabouts.

9.   Humorously anticipating a wrestling challenge from Mr. Bounderby, Mr. Harthouse decides to eat some meat as a way to fortify himself for the encounter.

10. Mr. Harthouse tells Sissy that he took advantage of Louisa's "father's being a machine…her brother's being a whelp…her husband's being a bear," adding that in doing so he "had no particularly evil intentions."

Suggested Essay Topics

1.   Gradgrind's new attitude toward his daughter is plain enough; he is full of remorse and tenderness. From their exchanges in Chapter 1, suggest what you think his daughter's attitude is toward him.

2.   Sissy's speeches to Mr. Harthouse have a theatrical, "worked up" quality unlike her usual manner but similar to that employed by other characters at other moments in the novel. Explain why her speeches have this quality and compare them to one other example of heightened or artificial speech.

3.   Explain why you think Mr. Harthouse gives in to Sissy.

Chapter 3: Very Decided

Summary

Mrs. Sparsit, ill from her late-night ordeal in the rain, pursues Bounderby to his hotel in London, tells him all she has seen and heard (and, no doubt, all that she imagines and fears), and faints dead away. After the usual restorative measures are applied, the two return by train to Coketown and proceed directly to Stone Lodge, where Bounderby bursts in upon Gradgrind demanding loudly to know where Louisa is. Told that she is right there in the house, Bounderby turns on Mrs. Sparsit and demands an apology for inventing stories. His housekeeper being incapable of speech, Bounderby escorts her out to the coach that conveyed them to Gradgrind's and tells her to return forthwith to the bank.

Alone with Gradgrind, Bounderby declares himself distinctly dissatisfied with what he calls his "treatment" by Louisa. Gradgrind ventures to say that there are "qualities in Louisa which have been harshly neglected and a little perverted." He goes on to recommend that Bounderby allow his wife to stay on at home, attended by Sissy. Bounderby, who swells and turns various shades of red as he listens to all this, launches into one of his familiar tirades. He is Josiah Bounderby of Coketown; he knows the town; knows its bricks, knows its works, knows its smoke, and knows its hands; they're real; Gradgrind's new talk of imaginative qualities is not; he knows what Gradgrind and his daughter really mean by it; they mean turtle soup and venison, and wanting to be set up in a coach and six. If that's what Louisa wants, Bounderby concludes defiantly, she had better get it from her father, because she will never have it from him. He tells Gradgrind that if Louisa is not at home with him by 12 o'clock the next day, he will send over her things and consider himself rid of her.

Bounderby returns home and goes to bed. Five minutes after noon the next day, Louisa not having reappeared, he gives directions to have his wife's clothing and other property returned to her, advertises his country retreat for sale, and resumes "a bachelor life."

Analysis

The resignation and sadness that Gradgrind now displays is offset by the unregenerate Bounderby in full cry. Bounderby's extraordinary energy, as well as his grotesque coarseness and absurdity, reach a kind of hateful climax here. Down to the ritual invocation of the turtle soup and venison, Dickens has Bounderby react to the disaster in his marriage as he might (and, in the case of Stephen Blackpool, does) some piece of impertinence, real or imagined, on the part of his employees. In effect, Bounderby fires his wife.

The comedy of the chapter—it is one of the funniest in the book—lies in Bounderby's "very decided" attitude, the insanely all purpose, insanely consistent nature of his responses, which are perhaps summed up in his "throwing on" his hat: the very gesture with which, so long ago, he accompanied Gradgrind into Coketown to find Sissy's father.

One satiric thrust stands out. It comes when Gradgrind reminds Bounderby that he took his daughter "for better or worse, for…" and Bounderby cuts him off. About this Dickens observes that "Mr. Bounderby may have been annoyed by the repetition of his own words to Stephen Blackpool." In fact there can be little question that Bounderby intends a formal separation, leading to a divorce; the speed with which he acts suggests that really he welcomes Louisa's departure. His thowing Mrs. Sparsit in Gradgrind's face as a high born lady who worships the very ground he walks on suggests that his housekeeper's triumph over her junior rival is, at least for now, complete.

Study Questions

1. What is it that Gradgrind is surprised Bounderby has missed?

2. Asked to speak, Mrs. Sparsit is reduced to what?

3. What does Mr. Bounderby call Mr. Harthouse?

4. What does Gradgrind entreat Bounderby, for his own sake and for Louisa's?

5. When Bounderby learns where Louisa is, he demands what from Mrs. Sparsit?

6. What does Mr. Bounderby advise his housekeeper to do when she returns to the bank?

7. Bounderby takes offense at Gradgrind's use of which common form of address?

8. According to Bounderby, what is the nature of the "incompatibility" between him and his wife?

9. Why does Bounderby declare he is glad that Gradgrind says he is being unreasonable?

10. What does Bounderby say he plans to tell anyone who asks him about his decision to part from Louisa?

Answers

1. Mr. Gradgrind is surprised that Mr. Bounderby has missed his letter.

2. Mrs. Sparsit is reduced to facial contortions, gestures at her throat, and finally, tears.

3. Mr. Bounderby calls Mr. Harthouse Mr. Gradgrind's "precious gentleman-friend."

4. Mr. Gradgrind asks Mr. Bounderby not to shout.

5. Mr. Bounderby demands an apology from Mrs. Sparsit.

6. Mr. Bounderby advises Mrs. Sparsit to put her feet in a tub of hot water, drink a glass of rum and butter, and go to bed.

7. Mr. Bounderby takes offense at Mr. Gradgrind's addressing him as "my dear Bounderby."

8. The nature of the incompatibility between his wife and himself is simply that she "don't properly know her husband's merits, and is not impressed with such a sense as would become her, by George! of the honour of his alliance."

9. Mr. Bounderby declares this because "when Tom Gradgrind, with his new lights, tells me what I say is unreasonable, I am convinced at once it must be devilish sensible."

10. Mr. Bounderby says he plans to tell people that "the two horses wouldn't pull together."

Suggested Essay Topics

1. Write a paper speculating about what would have to happen for Bounderby to undergo the same redemption apparently experienced by Gradgrind.

2. Imagine that Sissy stands in Mr. Gradgrind's place and must answer to Mr. Bounderby's anger. Having witnessed her performance with Harthouse, indicate how she might go about it.

Chapter 4: Lost
Chapter 5: Found

Summary

Despite his domestic difficulties, Mr. Bounderby remains intent on investigating the bank robbery. Hoping it will crack the case open, Mr. Bounderby has a "WANTED" poster for the missing Stephen Blackpool printed up in great black letters and pasted all over town before daybreak. The agitator Slackbridge denounces Blackpool with his usual overheated language, adding to his former denunciations of Stephen the names of thief and plunderer.

On the same evening that workers cluster around the posters in Coketown, the case suddenly erupts into the quiet confines of Stone Lodge. In the presence of her brother, Tom, who has arrived with Bounderby, Stephen Blackpool's old friend and "guardian angel" Rachael, her father, and Sissy, Louisa confirms the truth of Rachael's account of the visit she and Tom paid to Stephen the night he was fired.

Rachael says she has written Stephen about the charges against him and fully expects to see him return of his own free will in two day's time. Bounderby, who has treated Rachael with his customary tact, is less sure. Bidding everyone good night, he takes his leave, closely followed by Tom, whose farewells consist of a brief "Good night, father," and a scowl for his sister.

Rachael, who is terribly upset and cannot shake the thought that Louisa might have meant something more by her visit than simple charity, departs as well, but not before Sissy has discovered her address and promised to come over every evening to learn if there has been any news of Stephen. After Rachael leaves, Mr. Gradgrind lifts his head from his hands and muses aloud about whether the man Blackpool, whom he has never met, really is implicated in the crime. If he is not, he goes on in a worried way, might the real culprit know of the accusations? Where is he? Who is he? Just at that moment, Louisa and Sissy's eyes meet, a fearful knowledge passes between them and Louisa instantly places her finger on her lips. From that time on, as the days pass with no sign of Blackpool, they avoid mentioning his name in Gradgrind's presence.

True to her word, Sissy goes to Rachael every evening, and every evening learns that Blackpool has yet to be heard from. One night, out for a stroll that takes them by Bounderby's residence, they notice a coach come rattling up to Bounderby's door and hear the excited tones of Mrs. Sparsit ordering someone to come out. It is the old woman, firmly in the housekeeper's grip. A crowd of about 25 curious stragglers begins to gather as Mrs. Sparsit pulls her prey out of the carriage and starts dragging her inside.

With Rachael and Sissy behind her, and behind *them* the crowd of onlookers, Mrs. Sparsit calls out for Mr. Bounderby. Her employer, who had been meeting upstairs with Gradgrind and Tom, wonderingly descends the stairs to his drawing room. When he sees who Mrs. Sparsit has in custody, his face undergoes an extraordinary alteration. Of Mrs. Sparsit he unexpectedly demands to know what she means by this, and why she doesn't mind her own business? To everyone's amazement, it turns out that this old woman, Mrs. Pegler as she calls herself, far from being the looked for suspect in the robbery, is none other than Mr. Bounderby's own mother, loud in her cries of "My dear Josiah!" and "My darling boy!"

At this charged moment, Mr. Gradgrind, with a little of his old severity of manner, remarks that he is surprised that in her old age she has the audacity to claim Bounderby as her son, considering how she had deserted him in infancy. When Mrs. Pegler vehemently denies this, Mr. Gradgrind receives an inkling of the truth and asks whether she had not then allowed her son to grow up in the gutter? This provokes such a flood of denial and reminiscence of Bounderby's poor but decently cared for childhood, the love he received from both parents (his father dying when the boy was eight), the schooling he received, and the many kindnesses extended to him by others, including his first employer, that before she is done Bounderby stands revealed to all as the fraud and liar he is, a "self-made humbug."

Analysis

Mr. Bounderby's comeuppance is perhaps the most complete of any character in fiction. The simplicity of Dickens' conception, to suddenly confront the boastfully "self-made" man with a progenitor, an actual parent with a long memory and an active tongue, does nothing to take away from its comic genius. In line with its simplicity, perhaps, there is an archaic, punitive, almost medieval quality to Dickens' comedy here, pointed up in the reference to Bounderby's crestfallen state, as a bully who could not have looked "more shorn and forlorn, if he had had his ears cropped."

If there is nothing in the preceding chapter, or in the novel as a whole, that can quite compete with this amazing scene, still Gradgrind's coming as close as his newly functioning imagination can take him to the awful truth of his son's crime, has ironic force. Gradgrind's "where is he? who is he?" combined with the reference to his suddenly gray head—the compact, vigorous man in late middle age of his first appearances has, since his disillusionment, aged rapidly—suggests that Dickens sees in Gradgrind's situation elements of the tragic dilemma of an Oedipus or perhaps a Lear. The prolonging of the mystery of Blackpool's disappearance, and the various hints that Tom Gradgrind may actually have done away with Blackpool, show a skillful management of suspense on Dickens' part.

Sissy's joining forces with Rachael is a typical Dickensian development. At least as far as his good characters went, Dickens seemed to approve of the combination that he condemns among workers. They are less interesting together than either is paired with Louisa, because their type, the purely good, self-sacrificing angel of the household, is so similar.

Study Questions

1. Why does Mr. Bounderby think that, as a "commercial wonder," he is more admirable than Venus?

2. What sum is offered as reward for the arrest of Stephen Blackpool?

3. Why is the placard describing Blackpool being read aloud?

4. What resolution concerning Stephen Blackpool does Slackbridge propose?

5. What is young Tom doing while Bounderby pursues his investigations?

6. Why does Mrs. Sparsit cry out "It's a coincidence! It's a Providence!" when she spots Rachael and Sissy outside of Bounderby's house?

7. What "pension" has Bounderby supplied his mother with, in return for her silence?

8. Why do Sissy, Rachael, and Mr. Gradgrind think the lifting of suspicions against Mrs. Pegler bodes well for Stephen Blackpool?

9. Why has Tom been "plucked up" by a "forced spirit," and why does it "thrive" with him?

10. What truly dark imagining do both Sissy and Louisa entertain of Tom?

Answers

1. Mr. Bounderby is more admirable than Venus because he arose from the mud (of his poverty) and not, like the goddess, from the sea.

2. The award for the arrest of Stephen Blackpool is 20 pounds.

3. The placard is being read aloud to the workers who cannot read by their fellows who can.

4. Slackbridge proposes in his resolution that "Stephen Blackpool...having been already disowned by the community of Coketown, the same are free from the shame of his misdeeds, and cannot as a class be reproached with his dishonest actions!"

5. Tom moves about with Mr. Bounderby "like his shadow, assisting in all the proceedings."

6. Mrs. Sparsit knows that Rachael can positively identify the old lady in the coach as the mysterious old woman.

7. Bounderby has supplied his mother with 30 pounds a year.

8. The three think this because the old woman and Stephen had always been mentioned as associates; if she has nothing to do with the robbery, the chances increase that neither did he.

9. Tom has been "plucked up" by the nonappearance of Stephen Blackpool, and it thrives as his absence continues.

10. They suspect the possibility that Tom may have had Stephen "put out of the way" (killed), in order to permanently avert suspicion.

Suggested Essay Topics

1. What techniques does Dickens use to help increase the suspense as he heads into the home stretch of his narrative?

2. Examine the phrase "Bully of Humility" and show how it applies to the character of Mr. Bounderby, especially in Chapter 5.

Chapter 6: The Starlight

Summary

Rachael and Sissy Jupe spend a Sunday in the country just outside Coketown. Walking alone they come across a man's hat lying on the grass. Inside, written in his own hand, is the name Stephen Blackpool. Directly in front of the two women yawns the gaping mouth of an abandoned coal works, one of many that dot the landscape outside the city.

Sissy convinces Rachael not to give way entirely to lamentation, that there is a chance Stephen may still be alive at the bottom of the shaft. Marking the spot with a shawl, the two set off in different directions; Rachael back toward where they came, Sissy in another direction entirely, each hoping to raise the alarm about Stephen as they go.

Sissy comes across two men lying asleep by an engine house, wakes them, and manages to convey the nature of the emergency. One of the men has been lying in a drunken slumber, but when he grasps that a man has fallen down what his comrade shouts is the Old Hell Shaft, he dunks his head in a bucket of water and sobers quickly. Later he is at the head of those most useful at the site, as equipment and men and women from surrounding villages gather and a vigil begins.

Rachael returns with a surgeon. Few in the crowd think there is a chance that the fallen man might still be alive. Hours pass, the day turns to afternoon, then evening. Torches are brought out. Mr. Gradgrind and Louisa, Tom Gradgrind and Bounderby arrive, alerted by Sissy's message earlier in the day.

More equipment arrives, a windlass and bucket are improvised, and the crowd holds its collective breath as a volunteer—the sobered man Sissy found—descends into the depths of the shaft. He returns, the crowd cries out "dead or alive?" and a cheer goes up when he answers "alive." But he is hurt badly, the man adds over the noise, so badly he doesn't know how to bring him up without hurting him. The surgeon is called, there are consultations among the men, the windlass is lowered again, and finally there is raised up a "poor, crushed human figure."

It is Stephen. The surgeon does what he can—which is, chiefly, to have him covered. Stephen speaks at length to Rachael, briefly to Louisa, and finally to Mr. Gradgrind. He asks for his name to be cleared. How, asks Mr. Gradgrind. Ask your son, Stephen replies. He dies soon after, with Rachael holding his hand, as he is being carried across the open landscape.

Analysis

Stephen's dying speeches are a resumption of his old theme of the "muddle"; now the muddle includes the needless death that places like the Old Hell Shaft represent, in use or out of use alike. Dickens is not shy of using Stephen's last words to stir the conscience of his readers with what is almost a political speech, the sort of speech Dickens declines to give Slackbridge: "I ha' fell into a pit that ha' been wi' th' Fire-damp crueller than battle. I ha' read on 't in the public petition, as onny one may read, fro' the men that works in pits, in which they ha' pray'n the lawmakers for Christ's sake not to let their work be murder to 'em, but to spare 'em for th' wives and children that they loves as well as gentlefolk loves theirs. When it were in work, it killed wi'out need; when 'tis let alone, it kills wi'out need. See how we die an' no need, one way an' another—in a muddle—every day!" There is also the muddle of relations among the living, which has caused his fellow workers to mistake him and Bounderby to falsely accuse him.

Stephen speaks next of the star that he has been staring at from the bottom of the pit. It is associated in the chapter with the star that guided the magi to the cradle of the infant Jesus. "The God of the poor," Dickens pointedly adds. Dickens detested false religiosity as he detested almost nothing else, but especially on occasions such as Stephen's death, his own Christian feeling is plain.

The whole process of the rescue, starting from Rachael and Sissy's run for help, is made exciting and very real. Anyone who has ever been present at the scene of a disaster is likely to find Dickens' description rings true. It is interesting to note that the work the men do and the machinery they use to do the work are described in a way that celebrates both, which is certainly not true of descriptions of work and machinery elsewhere in the novel.

What Dickens seems to particularly admire is the spontaneous organization exhibited by the rescue party: making a ring around the shaft's edge, appointing people to keep it, choosing up volunteers, and so on. Notice, however, that although the effort is a collective one by the common people of the neighboring villages, social distinctions and deferences persist: the party from Coketown is permitted within the ring, and a surgeon (the one brought by Rachael) is given a supervisory function and is addressed with a "Sir."

Study Questions

1. Why do Sissy and Rachael, as they walk together in the countryside, avoid mounds of high grass?

2. Why do Sissy and Rachael not wish to look closely at Stephen's hat?

3. How does Sissy get Rachael to stop screaming?

4. Who holds the watch that tells how long the men have been down the shaft?

5. What can "practiced eyes" tell about the action of the windlass the first time it is brought up?

6. Which of the pitmen is the first to inform the crowd of Stephen's condition?

7. What has broken Stephen's fall?

8. Where was Stephen headed to before he fell?

9. What is Stephen's first utterance after he is delivered from the pit?

10. The litter on which he is being carried seems to Stephen to be moving in what direction?

Answers

1. Sissy and Rachael avoid these mounds because of stories that old pits are sometimes hidden under them.

2. The two women fear that the hat may be stained with blood, indicating that Stephen had met with foul play.

3. Sissy keeps repeating "Think of Stephen, think of Stephen" until Rachael calms down.

4. The surgeon announces how long the men have been down the shaft.

5. Mechanically-minded observers would know that the windlass was pulling in such a way as to have only one passenger.

6. The pitman who makes the announcement is the "sobered" man whom Sissy discovered asleep by the engine house.

7. Stephen has landed on a "mass of crumpled rubbish with which the pit was half choked up...his fall had been further broken by some jagged earth at the side."

8. Stephen was headed to Bounderby's summer house, intending to clear himself of the banker's charges.

9. The first thing Stephen says is Rachael's name.

10. Stephen has the impression that the litterbearers are moving in the direction of the star that has shone down on him for so long as he lay in the shaft.

Suggested Essay Topics

1. Christian imagery and language is employed in this chapter. State whether you think the usage is effective and compare it to a few chosen instances elsewhere in *Hard Times*.

2. The "sobered man" who is so active in the rescue operation is an example of a character in Dickens who, while so minor as not even to attain to the dignity of a name, is yet vivid and memorable. Suggest why you think Dickens chose to emphasize his participation by giving him such a leading role in the rescue effort.

Chapter 7: Whelp-Hunting

Summary

Tom Gradgrind stands by the Old Hell Shaft, next to Bounderby and a little apart from his father and sister. Sissy, seeing him there and watching him take in the fact that his father has been called to Stephen's side, leaves Rachael, steals up behind Tom and whispers something. The two confer briefly, and Tom leaves the scene without being seen.

As Sissy explains to Mr. Gradgrind, she had remembered where her father's old circus was at this time of year and had directed Tom to flee there and ask Mr. Sleary to take him in and hide him. Mr. Gradgrind, relieved that his son is in no immediate danger of arrest, takes heart when he realizes that Sleary's Circus is performing in a town not far from Liverpool, from where Tom could be shipped far away from England.

Using different routes to get there, Mr. Gradgrind, Louisa, and Sissy travel to Sleary's Circus. Sissy and Louisa arrive first. Sissy is warmly welcomed by Mr. Sleary and her old friends among the performers. Louisa asks after Tom; Mr. Sleary points out where he is on stage, completely disguised as a comic black servant. When later in the day Mr. Gradgrind arrives and enters the now empty circus ring, it is in this grotesque and ludicrous garb that his son appears before him, his face a mask of black greasepaint. After hearing the full story of the robbery, for which Tom says he alone was responsible, his father tells him he must be sent away from England as soon as possible. The family says its farewells. The elder Gradgrind tells him to "atone, by repentence and better conduct, for the shocking action you have committed, and the dreadful consequence to which it has led." Louisa opens her arms, but Tom spurns her.

As Mr. Sleary, the elder Gradgrind, Sissy, a crying Louisa, and a newly redisguised Tom, his face washed and dressed in a countryman's smock, leave the circus, a familiar figure suddenly runs into their midst and triumphantly collars Tom. It is Bitzer.

Analysis

In trying to have Tom spirited out of England by Sleary's Horse-Riders, Mr. Gradgrind and his party are undoubtedly engaged in frustrating justice; but, partly because Tom's rescue itself involves the humiliating punishment of his comic disguise, Dickens evidently thought his readers would not dwell on any legal niceties raised by Chapter 7. Modern readers are in any case more likely to be disturbed by Dickens' use of a racial stereotype, the comic black servant. Dickens means to show Tom as both ludicrous and abject, "blackened" by his evil actions, and for this the traditional figure of the stage "blackamoor" answered his purposes.

The reappearance of the circus at the conclusion of *Hard Times* is significant. Sleary's Horse-Riders, we remember, are a community devoted to the cultivation of the fancy, to art and creativity. At the beginning of the novel they had been regarded as at best a nuisance, at worst a set of dangerous vagabonds, by Mr. Gradgrind. Now he must rely on them to save his son. Mr. Sleary's generosity, his willingness to help the man he calls "Thquire," without once pressing him for any explanations or hinting at any reward, shows him to operate outside the realm of calculation and self-interest within which Bounderby, Bitzer, and until recently Gradgrind himself lived exclusively.

The confrontation between Mr. Gradgrind and his son is pure Dickens, and pure melodrama, all at once. There are the stagey lines of Gradgrind's farewell. There is the strangely compelling, pitiable, grotesque figure of Tom, the telling details of his monkey-like hands or his chewing on straw. There is the symbolic setting, with Gradgrind seated on a clown's stool in the middle of a deserted circus ring. And then there is the painful interchange between father and son, the former overcome by a sense of the disgrace this once "model child" has brought on himself (and on his father and his father's teachings), the latter feebly defiant, still able to use some of his father's old "statistical" habits of thought in his own defense, as when, in reply to his father's remark that he could not have been more shocked by the news of his son's deed than if a lightning bolt had fallen on him, he replies, "I don't see why not…so many people are employed in situations of trust; so many people, out of so many, will be dishonest. I have heard you talk, a hundred times, of its being a law. How can *I* help laws? You have comforted others with such things, Father. Comfort yourself!"

Contemplation of any such law as this offers no comfort, not anymore, not now that Gradgrind finds himself answerable to a new law: the law of the heart, a law whose least commandments now supersedes all his former economic determinism.

Study Questions

1. The title of Chapter 7, "Whelp-Hunting," refers to whom?

2. What does Gradgrind do as soon as he returns home from seeing Stephen Blackpool at the Old Hell Shaft?

3. What does Gradgrind tell Bounderby it is his duty to do?

4. At the outset of the family conference called by Gradgrind to discuss what to do about his son, what does Louisa say to encourage her father?

5. "Ten thousand pounds could not effect it," says Gradgrind. What is "it"?

6. Mr. Bounderby's "bullying vein of public zeal" might lead him to do what?

7. Where has Sleary's Horse-Riding set up?

8. Who sells the tickets for the circus?

9. Bitzer's long hard run has had what sort of singular effect on his appearance?

10. How does Mr. Sleary propose to get Tom to Liverpool?

Answers

1. The title "Whelp-Hunting" refers to Tom Gradgrind, first dubbed "the whelp" by Harthouse in Book 2, Chapter 2 and often so called by Dickens; "whelp" is a word of Anglo-Saxon

origin meaning the young offspring of dogs or meat-eating wild animals such as wolves or lions.

2. Gradgrind sends a message to Mr. Bounderby asking his son to come directly to Stone Lodge.

3. Gradgrind tells his old former ally that he considers it his duty to vindicate Stephen Blackpool's memory and declare the real thief.

4. Louisa tells her father he still has three young children (meaning her sister Jane and the two younger Gradgrind boys) who may be different from either Tom or herself.

5. Gradgrind says it would take more than 10,000 pounds to find Tom and spirit him out of the country in the short time remaining before he makes his son's act publicly known.

6. Mr. Bounderby might insist that his young brother-in-law be brought to justice, face a trial, and suffer punishment for his crime.

7. Sleary's Horse-Riding has set up in the marketplace of a small town more than 20 miles away from the town to which Sissy had directed Tom.

8. Master Kidderminster is the ticket taker.

9. Bitzer has "run himself into a sort of white heat, when other people run themselves into a glow."

10. Mr. Sleary intends to get Tom into a coach that will meet the mail train to Liverpool.

Suggested Essay Topics

1. Comment on the part played by railway travel in the novel. Restrict yourself to references to train travel in this chapter and no more than two or three other chapters in the novel.

2. Examine what Mr. Sleary says about Sissy's old friends, relate the stories he tells to themes in *Hard Times*, and indicate why you think Dickens has Mr. Sleary tell Sissy these stories.

Chapter 8: Philosophical
Chapter 9: Final

Summary

Bitzer stands before Gradgrind in the circus ring, holding Tom fast. Mr. Gradgrind, "broken and submissive," begins to appeal to him to let his son go. Each appeal is met with polite, "business-like," and "logical" refusal. No talk of "heart," no consideration of loyalty to his old master for the training that was bestowed upon him will induce him to release Tom. Bitzer has suspected Tom of the bank robbery from the first, and he's sure that if he delivers Tom over to Mr. Bounderby his employer would promote him to Tom's old place in the bank. No amount of money (Gradgrind asks him to name his sum) will change his mind. In calculating the matter—as he calculates all matters—he determines that his "compounding the felony" of Tom's crime by accepting money to let him go would not be so safe a course of action for him as returning Tom to Coketown and enjoying "improved prospects in the Bank."

Mr. Sleary, listening to all this, announces that he had no idea that Tom's wrongdoing was as serious as bank robbery. He will make sure nobody sees Tom and Bitzer leave for the station, but that's all he can do. Louisa and Gradgrind fall into despair when they hear this, but Sissy knows Sleary is up to something. As the company once more leaves the circus, Sleary draws her aside and excitedly whispers his plan. He will take Tom and Bitzer with him in a carriage drawn by one of his show horses, and he will have one of his trained dogs follow. The horse will, on command, start to dance about; Tom will jump out of the carriage and be picked up by Childers, driving a gig (a small carriage); if Bitzer tries to follow Tom, the dog will keep him and hold him.

The following morning Sleary arrives at the inn where Sissy, Louisa, and Gradgrind have all passed a suspenseful night. Ordering a glass of his invariable brandy and water, he is happy to inform them that the plan went off without a hitch, and Tom is probably at this moment on board a ship. Gradgrind offers him money, but Sleary refuses—for himself. Five pounds for Childers, a family man, a collar and a set of bells for the dog and the horse, dinner for the circus's company, the promise for the future of a

"bespeak" (a paid performance), and for himself a little more brandy and water would all be welcome and sufficient.

Sleary then asks for a parting word alone with Gradgrind. He tells him the story of Merrylegs, Sissy's father's dog, who had reappeared, blind and lame, among the circus people a little over a year ago, searched for Sleary, stood on his hindlegs, wagged his tail, and died. Sleary had thought of writing Sissy about the incident, feeling sure that it meant her father had died, but had decided against troubling her with the news. Calling the ladies back into the room Mr. Sleary makes his farewells, concluding with a repetition of his old credo, "People mutht be amuthed."

Some little time after these events, Bounderby sits at his dining room table, beneath his portrait, stewing. He is angry that Mrs. Sparsit has so far overreached herself as to meddle in his affairs and expose him to public ridicule, and he has made up his mind to fire her. Which, after some unpleasant words, he does. Standing in front of the fire, Mr. Bounderby thinks forward to the future.

That future holds, the narrator tells us, for Mrs. Sparsit a descent into pinched living with the unspeakable Mrs. Scadgers; for Bitzer, his hoped for promotion; for Bounderby, continuing prosperity, until in five year's time his sudden death, of a fit, on a Coketown street. For Mr. Gradgrind, it holds attempts to make his facts and figures serve Faith, Hope and Charity, and the consequent contempt of all his old political associates. For Rachael, it holds more work, cheerfully undertaken, and continuing care of a degraded, drunken woman (Stephen's wife) who can sometimes be seen in her company. For Tom it contains remorse and grief, and, in the course of a long voyage back to England, illness and death with his sister's name on his lips. For Sissy, it contains marriage and happy children. Not so for Louisa. For her the future holds a life-long dedication to learning about and understanding her "humbler fellow-creatures," and beautifying, as best she knows how, with "imaginative graces and delights" their lives of "machinery and reality."

Analysis

Everything Bitzer says in his interchange with Mr. Gradgrind he has been taught by the Gradgrind philosophy. In effect he is quoting back to Gradgrind all of Gradgrind's own arguments. Dickens handles the encounter so as to bring out all its irony. Gradgrind uses the language of entreaty and prayer; Bitzer responds with the language of argument and debate and calculation of motives. Gradgrind appeals to the emotions, to ideas of gratitude and loyalty; Bitzer responds with principles of political economy, with "self-interest."

The dialogue between Gradgrind and Bitzer is not the only "philosophical" portion of Chapter 8. Toward the end, when Sleary draws Gradgrind aside at the inn, Sleary launches into a characteristically humorous meditation on dogs and then relates the affecting story of Merrylegs, Sissy's father's old dog. His point, which is meant to directly counter Bitzer's "doctrines," is that there exists, in man and animal alike, a mysterious force of love, "not all Thelf-Interetht after all."

The "Dip into the Future" that the narrator provides in the final chapter of *Hard Times* is strikingly unlike the endings of Dickens' other novels. Of all the characters mentioned, only Sissy's future, with its promise of children, is of the "happily ever after" variety, and it is barely mentioned. The rest are consigned to varying degrees of unhappiness. Louisa's fate, which is explicitly contrasted to Sissy's, will be to engage in some sort of philanthropic endeavor. She will attempt to fulfill that "struggling disposition to believe in a wider and nobler humanity" that all her father's teachings were not able to eradicate from her heart.

Study Questions

1. As he is confiding his plans to Sissy, what does Sleary call Bitzer?

2. What does Mr. Gradgrind say is his last chance to soften Bitzer?

3. The reappearance of Merrylegs immediately suggests what to Mr. Sleary?

4. What is it that Sleary says people can't always be doing?

5. According to Mr. Sleary, a promise from Gradgrind to do what will more than balance his account with the circus?

6. How does Bounderby decide he can get the most glory out of his employment of his housekeeper?

7. What does Mrs. Sparsit ask Mr. Bounderby not to do as he begins to speak to her?

8. Mrs. Sparsit says the portrait of Mr. Bounderby has what advantage over the original?

9. What is the size of Lady Scadgers' establishment?

10. Louisa will be loved by all children, but by whose in particular?

Answers

1. Sleary calls Bitzer a "prethiouth rathcal" (precious rascal).

2. Mr. Gradgrind reminds Bitzer of the education he has received at his school.

3. When he sees Merrylegs, Mr. Sleary is sure that Sissy's father has died.

4. People, says Sleary, cannot always be made to learn, or always made to work.

5. Mr. Gradgrind will clear his debts to the circus by at some point in the future ordering a "bespeak."

6. Mr. Bounderby comes to the conclusion that firing Mrs. Sparsit will give him the most glory.

7. Mrs. Sparsit asks Mr. Bounderby not to bite her nose off.

8. The portrait has the advantage over its original of not possessing the power to speak, and "disgusting others."

9. Lady Scadgers' establishment is "a mere closet for one, a mere crib for two."

10. Sissy's children will love Louisa.

Suggested Essay Topics

1. Comment on the final lines of *Hard Times*. What does Dickens mean by his and his readers' "separate fields of action"? What course is he recommending his readers to follow?

2. The well-known English critic F. R. Leavis once called *Hard Times* a "moral fable." Indicate the evidence for this characterization in its two final chapters.

Sample Analytical Paper Topics

Topic # 1

In his representation of Coketown and what he calls the "fictions of Coketown," the ideas and attitudes that make it what it is, Dickens is doing more than offer incidental description of a city in the north of England. Dickens means Coketown to stand for the negative aspects of industrial society as a whole.

Outline

I.   Thesis Statement: *The city Dickens calls Coketown is meant to portray the pollution, ugliness, monotony, and health-destroying aspects of the new social order in England brought about by the industrial revolution and the social attitudes and prejudices that sustain it.*

II. The city is polluted, ugly, monotonous, and unhealthy

   A.   Pollution

      1.   Atmosphere thick with smoke and soot

      2.   Heaps of coal, litter, machinery

      3.   Dye from the cotton fabric is in the river and the canal is black and foul-smelling

   B.   Ugliness

      1.   The formless, unplanned nature of the city

    2.   The ostentation of Bounderby's residence

    3.   The meanness of Stephen's habitation and neighborhood

    4.   Neighborhoods half built up and half torn down by the railway

C. Monotony

    1.   The sameness of the work

    2.   The streets and buildings all built to be identical to one another

    3.   All public inscriptions painted alike

    4.   Sirens and bells each day

D. Health-destroying aspects of the city

    1.   Smoke-filled air

    2.   Smell of oil penetrating everywhere

    3.   Noise of the factories

    4.   Dangerous machinery

    5.   Abandoned coal pits

III. Ideas about society and prejudices circulated in Coketown by mill owners and men of business, political economists and Utilitarians, Parliamentary commissioners and schoolmasters

  A. Workers are machines

    1.   They can be measured exactly for their horsepower

    2.   They need enjoy no significant leisure time

    3.   No care should be expended on how they might re-create themselves

    4.   Workers' feelings are never to be consulted

  B. Human life holds no mysteries

    1.   Everything either is or should be the result of rational calculation

    2.   Workers are told never to ask questions and to take everything on faith

3. Material interest underlies all human actions

C. Factory workers are basically lazy and want money and luxury without working for it

    1. Bounderby's favorite saying about turtle soup and gold spoons

    2. The idea that real butter, fresh bread, sugar, and tea are extravagant luxuries when consumed by workers

IV. Conclusion: Dickens' Coketown represents the negative aspects of the industrial revolution, the social order it created, and the ideas and attitudes that sustained it.

Topic # 2

Sissy Jupe's influence as a character

Outline

I. Thesis Statement: *Sissy Jupe has a strong influence on the events in the novel and on the emotional lives of those to whom she is attached.*

II. Influences events

A. Gets rid of Harthouse

    1. Goes to him in a self-appointed capacity as Louisa's ambassador

    2. Tells him he must never see her again

    3. Is not put off by his fine, gentlemanly airs

    4. Is sure of herself throughout the encounter

B. Helps discover Blackpool

    1. Is first to spread word that Blackpool has fallen down Old Hell Shaft

C. Helps Gradgrind's son escape from England

    1. Has idea of contacting Mr. Sleary and enlisting his help in disguising and spiriting Tom away from his pursuers

2. Accompanies Louisa to the circus

III. Influence on characters' emotional lives

A. In childhood, tries to comfort her despairing father

1. Reads to her father from his favorite stories

2. Rubs his body with the restoring "nine oils"

3. Is always cheerful around him

B. Gives Louisa hope

1. Does not condemn Louisa for the failure of her marriage

2. Remains steadfast in her loyalty and friendship to Louisa

C. Helps Gradgrind toward his redemption as a person capable of feelings

1. Shows a good example to him by caring for people in his household

2. Is always pleasant and diffuses gentleness at Stone Lodge

3. Makes him see how mistaken he was about her

D. Is a companion to Rachael

1. Helps Rachael cope with Stephens' disappearance

2. Prevents Rachael from flinging herself down Old Hell Shaft

3. Is there for Rachael when the worst is confirmed

IV. Conclusion: Despite her humble origins, meekness, simplicity, and complete dependence on Gradgrind's charity, Sissy turns out to be nothing less than the Gradgrind family's savior.

Topic #3

The characters in *Hard Times* fall into two categories, with two exceptions.

Outline

I.   Thesis Statement: *The characters in* Hard Times *are either capable of unselfishly sympathizing with other people's sufferings or they are selfish and calculating, with two exceptions—Gradgrind and Louisa.*

II. Selfish characters incapable of sympathy

   A. Bounderby

      1. Does not care about the difficulties faced by the people who work for him, in particular Blackpool

      2. Has no conception of his wife's unhappiness

      3. Shows remarkable tactlessness on the occasion of visiting Sissy's father to tell him that Sissy can't go to school any longer

   B. Bitzer

      1. Puts his own mother in a workhouse

      2. Cannot be appealed to on the grounds of loyalty or feeling

      3. Refuses to let Tom Gradgrind escape justice

   C. Tom Gradgrind

      1. Makes his sister marry a man she doesn't love for his own convenience

      2. Is nevertheless ungrateful toward his sister

      3. Shows no remorse for hurting his family

III. Characters who are capable of unselfish sympathy

   A. Sissy Jupe

      1. Is Rachael's companion and source of comfort when Blackpool disappears

      2. Intervenes for Tom and helps him

      3. Attends the sick and dying mother of Louisa

 B. Rachael

  1. Takes care of Stephen's drunken wife, her old friend

  2. Has pity and concern for Stephen

 C. Mr. Sleary

  1. Makes sure that Sissy really wants to go to Gradgrind's

  2. Knows the troubles and joys of all his employees

  3. Shows sympathy for Sissy's father

  4. Shows sympathy for Sissy

IV. Louisa and Gradgrind are the exceptions

 A. Gradgrind undergoes a change

  1. For the first two-thirds of the novel he is unsympathetic, cold, and uncaring

  2. Louisa reappears to expose his radical deficiency as a father

  3. From that moment on he is a changed man struggling to find ways to act differently

 B. Louisa alternates between being capable of sympathizing with others and being incapable of doing so

  1. Like her father can be cold and haughty

  2. But is devoted to her brother

  3. Shows sympathy for Blackpool and goes to his lodgings to give him money

  4. In the future, Dickens says that she will not be a mother, but she will devote herself to caring for others in humanitarian work

V. Conclusion: All characters in the novel are either capable of sympathy with others or incapable of sympathy, with two exceptions: Louisa has moments of both, but only Gradgrind is able to undergo a transformation.

Topic #4

Ridicule can be a powerful instrument in the hands of a skill-ful writer. Write an essay exploring the uses of ridicule in *Hard Times*.

Outline

I. Thesis Statement: *In the novel* Hard Times *Dickens uses ridicule to entertain the reader and to puncture inflated language, attack ideas, and expose attitudes he dislikes.*

II. Punctures inflated language

    A. Mrs. Sparsit's genteel speech

        1. Calling her salary an "annual compliment"

        2. Being unwilling to mention that Bitzer snores

        3. Terms she uses for her employer

    B. Slackbridge's rhetoric

        1. Speeches prolific with cliché and dead metaphors

        2. His addressing everyone as his friend

        3. Appeal to hatred and resentment

III. Attack ideas

    A. Mr. Gradgrind's theory of education

        1. Force feeding children a steady diet of facts

        2. Cultivating the intellect at the expense of the emotions

        3. Forbidding any indulgence in fancy

        4. Not allowing imaginative literature of any kind

    B. Mr. Bounderby's attitude toward his employees

        1. Belief that they all want "to be set up in a coach and six, and to be fed on turtle soup and venison, with a gold spoon"

        2. High-handed dismissal of Blackpool

        3. Automatic suspicion of Blackpool

       4.   Belief that Coketown's workers are the happiest who ever lived, and Coketown's work the easiest

  C. The "Harthouse Philosophy"

       1.   Life is boring

       2.   No opinion is worth more than another

       3.   Benevolence and social concern is meaningless

       4.   "Whatever Will Be, Will Be"

IV. Expose attitudes

  A. Mr. Bounderby's upstart attitudes

       1.   The made-up stories of his abandonment

       2.   His "braggart humility"

       3.   Boasting of his lack of manners

  B. Mrs. Sparsit's family pride

       1.   Her references to the Powlers and Lady Scadgers

       2.   Condescending air toward everyone despite the lowliness of her present station in life

V. Conclusion: Dickens uses ridicule relentlessly and effectively to mock a variety of his characters and their outlooks.

SECTION SIX

Bibliography

Altick, D. Richard. *Victorian People and Ideas: A Companion for the Modern Reader of Victorian Literature.* New York: W.W. Norton, 1973.

Dickens, Charles. *Hard Times: A Norton Critical Edition.* Edited by George Ford and Sylvere Monod. New York: W.W. Norton, 1966.